THE I AM IN ME

THE I AM IN ME

2ND EDITION

TEKISHA D. WIMBUSH

 J Merrill Publishing, Inc.
434 Hillpine Drive
Columbus, OH 43207
www.JMerrill.pub

Library of Congress Control Number: 2022913373
ISBN-13: 978-1-954414-50-1 (Paperback)
ISBN-13: 978-1-954414-49-5 (eBook)

Book Title: The I Am In Me
Author: Tekisha D. Wimbush

CONTENTS

ACKNOWLEDGMENTS

Our Lord and Savior Jesus Christ. Loving Memory of "MaMa" grandmother Jennie Ruth Jackson that led to my business ownership of MaJennie Creations LLC, to my husband Bishop Willie James Wimbush Jr., to my mother Pastor Shawyl R. Williams, to my children Jasemine, Jaden, and Jahdon. To my grandchildren, my Church: Church of the Reform Church of Love Family, to Sister 2 Sister Women's Focus Group and COTRCOL Women's Forum- Founder Mother Gannie Jackson and to all of my family and friends that inspire and motivate me to be a better self.

FOREWORD

On April 28, 2016 I began to ask a question of God, myself and my husband: "How and what can be done to help 'Women' move past being 'beat up,' broken, hurt, bitter, angry, unforgiving, scorned, scarred, victimized and confused? How can we 'move forward' from this 'captivity' of emotions?" This form of mental bondage has symptomized itself into physical, emotional and mental, visible manifestations, crippling and stagnating this beautiful population of virtuosity- this "fearfully and wonderfully" made species that we call 'Women' (Psalm 139:14).

Earlier that day God provided me with a word: I was aligned for a purpose for a time such as now, and I would Bridge Gaps. Have you ever found yourself questioning or petitioning God anew and He has already provided you with the answer just as clear and profound, but our "finite minds" zoom right past the Lord's response, or the answer is incomprehensible, and our mortal mind does not want to accept or comprehend? Well, that is exactly what happened! Hours later my mind caught up with my deliverance and, as

Peter writes in the Book of Acts, "While he was yet speaking," (Acts 10:44), the wheels of my mind began turning.

In conversing with my pastor, God said, "Women's Focus Group!" With no name or politically correct thesis, philosophy or foundation, I said, "Lord, when? How? What to do? No time." But you know that if God calls you to it, He will equip, qualify, and guide you through it! Just smile and keep on GOING! I am sure by now your thoughts have been moved and your memory has been jogged at the countless times this has happened to you! Well, I decided to go with it since there is NO failure in God and FAITH is what FAITH does! "Now Faith" (Hebrew 11:1).

May 5, 2016, I pondered a Name for this women's focus group. As I was speaking with my daughter, Jasemine, the name hit me: "Jasemine," I screamed, "the name is Sister2Sister." I'm sure our philosophy (school of thought) coincides! For we are sisters in the Body of Christ and we are helpers one to another. Building new found healthy relationships with Christ is our Center and our foundation! We are Women, the female human being, as distinguished from a girl or a man (Dictionary.com). The rib taken from the side of Adam (Genesis 2:21-23). We are the carriers of life. Remember, the women carried, life, truth, deliverance, the Word, our Savior, all in her womb. For it was woman who birthed "Destiny" and delivered the "Promise"!

The Mission of this Sister2Sister women's focus group, built upon a holistic perspective, mind, body, soul, is to provoke women to "Rise Up" and "Move" out of fragmented mind sets, isolated and dark places of being; taking hold of, binding up and sending back to the pits of hell emotive thoughts and feelings of "Beat Up, Brokenness, Hurt, Bitterness, Anger, Unforgiveness, Untrusting, Scorned, Scarred, Victimized, out of touch of their own Purpose, defining their destinies and living out the "Promises of God." This movement is for women to "aspire and to inspire" both healthy and positive change, development and growth fostering a "Holistic Perspective and Approach" conquering battles of loneliness, jealousy, discouragement, frustration, low self-esteem, unworthiness, poverty, lack of education, poor communication, fear, inability to think and process thoughts of emotions, and breaking through barriers of depression and mental instability. No longer will they bow down and give up being defined by poorly exhibited content of character. Rather, they will be the "Virtuous Women" God designed and "Chose." "For with God all things are Possible," (Matthew 19:26). This movement of sisterhood recognizes that before we were mothers, wives, baby mothers, girlfriends, side chicks, main girl crushes, (victims), rape victims, child abused victims, domestic violence victims, mental abused victims, mental illness/physical illness victims, we were a child of God of our Creator, and then "Women," the carrier of life!

The formation of Sister2Sister Women's Focus Group led to the creation of this self-help book, a tool to motivate and to encourage others to be a better self, filled with life applicable scriptures and exercises that apply to our own life journey.

Looking at life with new eyes to renew our minds and build new behavioral outcomes, as John C. Maxwell articulates, it's time to "SWITCH." In effort to progress to where God is requiring of me:" to "SWITCH" from I am not where I should be, we will no longer make excuses in God. It is Time to SWITCH! (John C Maxwell).

Stop Wasting Invaluable Time Contemplating Hinderance time out for SIN (Self-Inflicted-Nonsense).

Simply I Am _____ Me!

1
———

I AM ME: A VIRTUOUS WOMAN
OF GOD

A WOMAN OF INTEGRITY

*V*irtuous - Simply, I am _____ Me!
      The Question Posed: Who can find a Virtuous
Woman? Proverbs 31:10

Virtuous

_____
_____
_____

Chastity

_____
_____
_____

Modesty

_____
_____
_____

Integrity

_____

_____

_____

The fear of the Lord is the beginning of "Wisdom."

The fear of the Lord is the beginning of "Wisdom" (Proverbs 9:10). The Bible will be our foundational guide, as with other books, tools, instruments, schools of thought, theories, and quotes we will build. Then, using various modalities of interventions, spiritual affirmations, arts, crafts, games, ice breakers, trips, retreats, community events, community resources, cooking, etc., in efforts to accomplish the mission of Jesus Christ in our Sister2Sister Women's Focus Group we must reach the masses while yet Building up My Sister!

The Virtuous Women Exercise

The Bible says, "Examine yourselves, whether ye be in the faith; prove your own selves" (2nd Corinthians 13:5). The long self-examination window often frightens individuals. Why? Because you do not like what you see, it is always easier to pick the flaws and imperfections in others rather than the self. Part of this reflection requires you to totally focus on yourself. Yes, pick yourself apart. Find out the good and bad characteristics in an effort to rebuild a healthier Christ-like self. Remember that only the "pure in heart will see God" (Matthew 5:8). Take a moment to review our foundational scripture leading with a question:

Is the painted picture of Lemuel's writings in the proverb of the virtuous woman?

_____

_____

In examination, reflecting on the scriptures, where are you in the verses?

_____

_____

Please journalize your findings. Assessment is always the initial
step to problem resolution.

_____

_____

_____

_____

_____

_____

Virtuous - having or showing high moral standards: synonyms: righteous, good, pure, whiter than white, saintly, (especially of a woman) chaste.
  according to Dictionary.com

Proverbs 31:10-31 (KJV)

*10 Who can find a virtuous woman? for her price is
far above rubies.*

*11 The heart of her husband doth safely trust in her,
so that he shall have no need of spoil.*

*12 She will do him good and not evil all the days of
her life.*

*13 She seeketh wool, and flax, and worketh willingly
with her hands.*

*14 She is like the merchants' ships; she bringeth her
food from afar.*

*15 She riseth also while it is yet night, and giveth
meat to her household, and a portion to her
maidens.*

*16 She considereth a field, and buyeth it: with the
fruit of her hands she planteth a vineyard.*

*17 She girdeth her loins with strength, and
strengtheneth her arms.*

*18 She perceiveth that her merchandise is good: her
candle goeth not out by night.*

*19 She layeth her hands to the spindle, and her hands
hold the distaff.*

*20 She stretcheth out her hand to the poor; yea, she
reacheth forth her hands to the needy.*

*21 She is not afraid of the snow for her household: for
all her household are clothed with scarlet.*

*22 She maketh herself coverings of tapestry; her
clothing is silk and purple.*

*23 Her husband is known in the gates, when he
sitteth among the elders of the land.*

*24 She maketh fine linen, and selleth it; and
delivereth girdles unto the merchant.*

*25 Strength and honour are her clothing; and she
shall rejoice in time to come.*

*26 She openeth her mouth with wisdom; and in her
tongue is the law of kindness.*

27 She looketh well to the ways of her household, and

eateth not the bread of idleness.

28 *Her children arise up, and call her blessed; her husband also, and he praiseth her.*

29 *Many daughters have done virtuously, but thou excellest them all.*

30 *Favour is deceitful, and beauty is vain: but a woman that feareth the Lord, she shall be praised.*

31 *Give her of the fruit of her hands; and let her own works praise her in the gates.*

What are your thoughts about these scriptures?

_____

_____

_____

_____

_____

_____

_____

_____

_____

_____

_____

_____

_____

_____

_____

_____

_____

_____

_____

_____

_____

_____

2

CHOOSING TO BE HAPPY

*I*t is a rich sense of well-being that comes from knowing you can deal productively and creatively with all that life offers, both the good and the bad; it is knowing your internal self and responding to your actual needs rather than the demands of others and a deep sense of engagement, living in the moment and enjoying life's "bounty."

The author outline (nine) parameters of happiness:

1. Intention: The active desire and commitment to be happy and the fully conscious decision to choose happiness over unhappiness.
2. Accountability: The choice to create the life you want to live, assume full personal responsibility for your actions, thoughts, and feelings, and emphatic refusal to blame others for your own unhappiness.
3. Identification: The ongoing process of looking deep within yourself to assess what makes you uniquely happy apart from what you're told by others should make you happy.

4. Centrality: The non-negotiable insistence on making that which creates happiness central in your life.

5. Recasting: The choice to convert the problems into opportunities and challenges and to transform trauma into something meaningful, important, and a source of emotional energy.

6. Options: The decision to approach life by creating multiple scenarios to be open to new possibilities and to adopt a flexible approach to life's journey.

7. Appreciation: The choice to appreciate deeply your life and the people in it and to stay in the present by turning each experience into something precious.

8. Giving: The choice to share yourself with friends and community and to give to the world without expecting a "return."

9. Truthfulness: The choice to be honest with yourself and others in an accountable manner by not allowing societal, corporate, or family demands to violate your internal contract.

Happiness: A definitive state of emotions, temporal by means of defining the parameters above, is an instrument to assume the state of happiness. One must agree that the state of happiness varies uniquely from individual to individual, understanding that one's circumstances often depict one's emotional state of happiness; thus, the parameters presented state that one has to choose happiness.

The Bible defines happy as "contented, joyous, fortunate." The understanding of true and lasting happiness comes from the Lord. The author of the short couplets recognized as proverbs, Proverbs of Solomon, writes, *"Treasures of wickedness profit nothing: but righteousness delivereth from death," Proverbs 10:2.* From this scripture, we understand that the state of happiness is a choice and individuals at times bring the state of unhappiness upon themselves by way of choices, (wrong choices). With clarity of decision-making, we must make sound, rational, well-informed decisions that are in the will of God in an effort to be centered and aligned with God's will to achieve lasting happiness, happiness that is not depicted by ever-changing feelings. Only then will one understand JOY given by God, which no man can take away. *For the Joy of the Lord is your strength (Nehemiah 8:10).* David found the secret to joy that is on the inside of you. According to *Psalm 16:9, Therefore my heart is glad, and my glory rejoiceth: my flesh also shall rest in hope.* Choose to be "Happy" and live to experience the joy of the Lord!

Happiness Joy Unhappy Joyless

Circle all the words you choose listed above and speak these words over your life.

_____

_____

_____

_____

_____

_____

_____

_____

_____

_____

_____

_____

_____

_____

_____

_____

3

TRUST

---

*Candle: A long, usually slender piece of tallow or wax with an
embedded wick that is burned to give light.*

---

*uickly list three scriptures regarding candles, the
representation of light. Here's one: "Let us continue to
strive to be that light that shines on a hill and cannot be
hidden," Matthew 5:14.*

1. _____
2. _____
3. _____

*Six months into the conception of Sister2Sister, we have shared
some monumental milestones of bonding and growth. The journey
must continue! For I AM my sister's keeper! I AM. We understand
that God is I AM and that all things are possible with Him! Recorded
in Exodus, the book of the "Coming Out," God chose Moses as leader
of the Children of Israel to bring them out of bondage, out of the land*

of Egypt, and deliver them to a land that flowed with milk and honey, known as the "Promised Land"!

"And God said unto Moses, 'I Am That I Am.' And He said, 'Thus shalt thou say unto the children of Israel,' I Am hath sent me unto you." (Exodus 3:14). God is yet sending his leaders messengers of Christ to compel and to deliver his people back to Him from the snares of bondage. There are many twists and turns in this story, including the continued bondage that Israel rigorously found themselves back in time after time. Have you ever been there? We all have!

The chosen people of God help us to understand that slavery (bondage) is a state of mind. True "Freedom" can only come to those who have been mentally liberated, to those that are truly "TRUSTING" in the Lord. Solomon's famous Proverb (3:5-7) says, *"Trust in the Lord with all of thine heart; and lean not unto thy own understanding. In all of thy ways acknowledge Him and he shall direct thy paths."* So, let's add "Trust" to our mission-driven purpose as a barrier to overcome, that we must have trust applied belief in God, that He knows what is best for us. So, we must exchange our thoughts and ways for His. Jesus affirms this in the new testament, *Matthew 6:33, "But seek ye first the kingdom of God, and his righteousness; and all these things shall be added unto you."*

Will you take a moment and define the word T R U S T?

_____

_____

_____

Share a brief testament of how your T R U S T is or is not, or had been, an issue or factor for you. Please include a method of overcoming.

_____
_____
_____
_____
_____
_____

Please group with at least two people. **For where two or three are gathered together in My name, there am I in the midst of them,** Matthew 18:20, and declare by way of verbal shout **"I Will Trust in The Lord."**

_____
_____
_____
_____
_____
_____
_____
_____
_____
_____
_____
_____
_____
_____
_____
_____
_____
_____
_____

4

RE-CENTERING YOUR FOCUS

*F*ocus *is the ability to focus one's thoughts or to concentrate to direct one's attention or efforts*
Understanding the true definition of the word FOCUS, there is a pre-distinction that the sense of one's FOCUS can sometimes get out of line or perhaps become unclear, leading one to be unfocused.

UNFOCUSED: Lacking a clear purpose or direction. I am sure the percentile rate for the prevalence of losing FOCUS on envisioned thoughts, plans, goals, or ideals is high. If you are reading this, I am sure at one time or another, your Focus was "unclear, cloudy, or blurry to the vision of thought," if you will. How about just being visually impaired? Many circumstances come and cause one to lose their FOCUS. Let's look at some reasons._____, _____, _____. We will review three. We find that Eve lost her focus in the beginning, according to 2nd **Corinthians 11:3:** "**But I fear, lest by any means, as the serpent beguiled (deceived) Eve through his subtle (cunning), so your minds should be corrupted from the simplicity that is in Christ.**" It appears that Eve lost her focus by listening to the devil.

Genesis 3:4-5 (And the serpent said to the woman, Ye shall not surely die: For God know that in the day ye eat thereof, then your eyes shall be opened, and ye shall be as gods, knowing good and evil).

(1.) This act of listening caused Eve to become confused and to lose focus on God and what he had spoken to her and the instructions he had given, leading to disobedience and sin.

(2.) The Children of Israel were to inherit the land that flowed with milk and honey God promised to Abraham, Isaac, and Jacob. For several reasons of loss of FOCUS, this eleven-day journey took 40-plus-one years. Let us look at one of the UNFOCUSED moments revealed in Numbers 13:25-29.

> *And they returned from searching of the land after forty days. And they went and came to Moses, and to Aaron, and to all the congregation of the children of Israel, unto the wilderness of Paran, to Kadesh; and brought back word unto them, and unto all the congregation, and shewed them the fruit of the land. And they told Him, and said, we came unto the land whither thou sentest us, and surely it floweth with milk and honey; and this is the fruit of it. Nevertheless the people be strong that dwell in the land, and the cities are walled, and very great: and moreover, we saw the children of Anak there. The Amalekites dwell in the land of the south: and the Hittites, and the Jebusites, and the Amorites, dwell in the mountains: and the Canaanites dwell by the sea, and by the coast of Jordan.*

Observation would tell us that the spies made several excuses and often reflected on the negative instead of the positive. All correlate to feelings that manifested as thoughts of Fear. Fear caused the Israelites to lose FOCUS on what God had already promised and had done for them! Note, do not allow potential issues to blind you from God's promise never to forsake you, to be a present help, to direct thy path, and to order your steps! Last but not least:

(3.) After a great personal victory, Samson was both physically and emotionally drained.

> And he was sore athirst, and called on the Lord, and
> said, Thou hast given this great deliverance into
> the hand of thy servant: and now shall I die for
> thirst, and fall into the hand of the
> uncircumcised)?
>
> — JUDGES 15:18

It appears that Samson lost FOCUS after his personal victory due to taking the FOCUS off God and reflecting it upon Himself. By equation, the word *Pride* comes to mind. One must remember that after a draining victory when you think there is peace and safety, sudden destruction lays waiting for your time of vulnerability. Hence, "STAY FOCUSED ON GOD!" The one thing that is beautiful in its own way is that there are corrective lenses for those struggling with their sight or insight! The ability to FOCUS, contrary to popular belief, one can, by desire, regain or re-center their FOCUS! There are avenues and ways of escape that God has blessed us with to re-center our FOCUS.

Thoughts:

_____

_____

_____

We know that obedience to Him and His word is better than sacrifice (1st Samuel 15:22). We know that he has not given us the spirit of fear. Still, of power, love and of a sound mind, 2nd Timothy 1:7. Keeping your mind stayed on God, for he promised to keep you in perfect peace, Isaiah 26:3. We understand better that FOCUS in or on GOD is imperative, for your adversary lurks to steal, kill, and destroy. Still, the rock of our salvation, that center of hope, a present help in the time of trouble, came that we might have life and life more abundant *(John 10:10.)*

Let's re-center our Focus, building upon those things that are eternal, for we know that only what you do for Christ will last.

If you fail the first time, do not lose FOCUS because of distractions; get back up, Re-center your SELF and try it again!

When situational occurrences happen within your life, here are some options: Let it destroy you, define you, or strengthen you!

Remember, if God be for us, then who can be against us? All things are working for your GOOD. There is nothing impossible through God! Re-center Your FOCUS!

_____

_____

_____

_____

_____

_____

_____

_____

_____

_____

_____

_____

_____

_____

5

IT'S A NEW DAWN, IT'S A NEW DAY, AND I'M FEELING GOOD. START A NEW DAY!

"It's a New Dawn, it's a New Day. It's a New Life for Me and I'm Feeling Good!"

— *ANTHONY NEWLEY AND LESLIE BRICUSSE*

*T*he lyrics alone are impactful. The songwriters' states claim artistically by way of ownership to their feelings, thoughts, or state of mind. Professing that it is a "New Day," I am sure we could speculate that the previous day may have or may not have been good or not good at all. However, the writer understands that dawn has come, the daylight has arisen. For whatever I dealt with yesterday, it is yesterday's news!

Because the aftermath is "It is a New Dawn and a New Day," "I have a New Life for me, and I choose to feel good!"

Ironically, these lyrics are parallel to the testament of David that ***"Weeping may endure but for a night,"*** ***"but Joy*** *comes in the Morning!" (Psalm 30:5.)* "It's a New Dawn, it's a New Day.

It's a New Life for me and I'm Feeling Good."

Poetically scripted, the psalmist translates that you may have to cry sometimes, shedding a ray of light amidst disparity. That gives hope in knowing that weeping does not last always, but for a night and at the breaking of dawn on this day, my joy shall be restored.

These two descriptions of artistry are ways of expression. The songwriter, is definitively a person or persons who write the words or music or both for popular songs, sometimes through self-experiences of life or vicariously lived through the eyes of others, creatively, mentally, and emotionally connected in a rhythm of thoughts, compositions of lyrics and sounds are created. The book of Psalm is poetically written by way of outward expression to convey praise, worship, and confession unto God. The psalmists wrote in outward expressions of their human experiences. Negating cliché expressions, they portrayed intimate thoughts of emotion from the raw depths of their hearts and souls. In some cases, crying out to God by way of confessions of sins, their doubts and fears, and requests for help in times of trouble.

Intimacy is **KEY** in these expressive mannerisms, for the development of intimacy is a process of deep understanding or knowledge of something. In this case, we are speaking of God. Expression of intimacy with God denotes a close, familiar, and usually affectionate or loving personal relationship with Him. Who Knows You Better? Intimacy with God is reflective of Moses' writing in *Deuteronomy 6:5. "Thou shalt love the Lord your God with all thine heart, with all thy soul and with all thou might. (Matthew 22:37) reflects, "Jesus said unto Him, Thou shalt love the Lord thy God with all thy heart, and with all thy soul, and with all thy mind." "This is the first and great commandment."* Innately, we were created to praise and worship God, and God only withholding nothing. *"Let everything that has breath praise the Lord." "Praise ye the Lord." (Psalm 150:6)*

(8) Things to Optimistically Focus Upon and Remember to say and live from day to day:

1. Your Good Days Do Outweigh Your Bad Days
2. Don't Complain
3. For Weeping May Endure for a Night
4. But Joy Comes in the Morning
5. It is a New Dawn,
6. It is a New Day,
7. It is a New Life for Me and
8. I am Feeling Good!

Share Reflective Thoughts on Yesterday:

_____
_____
_____

Share Reflective Thoughts on Today:

_____
_____
_____

For "Death and life are in the power of the tongue" (Psalm 18:21). It is a New Dawn! It is a New Day! It is a New Life for Me and I am Feeling Good!" even as the scripture professes, *"Not boasting in oneself but in the Lord." (Proverbs 27:1) Boast not thyself of tomorrow; for thou knows not what a day may bring forth.* One Day at a Time, I will take each day as it comes. So we find that we should not worry about tomorrow. (Matthews 7:34) "Take therefore no thought for the morrow: for the morrow shall take thought for things of itself. Sufficient unto the day is the evil thereof."

Start a New Day

Journalize your intimate thoughts as a psalmist artistically unto God, for he is "our refuge and strength; a very present help in the time of trouble" (Psalm 46:1).

_____

_____

_____

_____

_____

_____

_____

_____

_____

_____

_____

_____

_____

_____

_____

_____

_____

_____

_____

_____

_____

_____

_____

_____

_____

_____

_____

_____

_____

_____

6

THE WAR BEGINS: WOMEN TO WARRIORS
"EQUIPPED AND IGNITED TO SERVE"

re you ready for the war?
Consider, when we look at a Godly woman, an adult human female, it represents well the kingdom of God, her husband, and her children. **"Her character is known beyond the home or the church. She positively influences others and her influence is felt in the community."** (Davis, 2012, p.41)

The writer of *Proverbs 31:10 (Lemuel) asks a question: Who can find a virtuous woman?* One who is true, strong, creative, compassionate, resourceful, God-fearing, and inspirational, a woman of Faith. A good wife, a mother, a servant, a homemaker, an entrepreneur, skilled and crafty. She is patient, kind, loving, respectful, wise, intelligent, a woman of integrity. *"Whitney Houston and Chaka Khan said, "I'm Every Woman."* The writer describes her character, not focusing on her looks or outer appearance. While we know all women should look good, your race, culture, ethnicity, height, or size does not define a virtuous woman. Still, her *character* is what is beautifully described as "picture perfect."

In striving to be "Every Woman," she is often "called to duty." She must have a kindling of *fire down on the inside* and the ability to ignite when necessary without doubt and go to war if she must. A virtuous woman is equip*ped. "She is ignited, and she is ready to serve."*

The question is, are you ready for the War?

We understand that a warrior is a serviceman, a brave, strong, experienced fighter who goes to battle in a war. They are armed, dangerous, and ready for conflict. The word WAR is a verb meaning there will be opposing engagement; there will be opposition.

When observing the character of the servant Hannah, the mother of Samuel, we find that she was in a WAR, 1st Samuel, written by Samuel (because I have asked Him of the Lord). Samuel was the last judge of Israel. His writing captures the reign and downfall of Saul, the first king, the chosen preparation of David. Samuel gives historical events of Israel's transition from a theocracy (led by God), to a Monarchy (led by a king), against God's plan for Israel. Also, against God's plan was a time of polygamy (the practice custom of having more than one wife or husband at the same time). During this Old Testament time, a childless woman was considered a failure and ridiculed socially as an embarrassment to her husband. Hannah was Barren, "unable to give birth to children." Like Hannah, we all sometimes, as individuals, experience a stage of "Barrenness," unable to give "Birth" to our Destiny. Our future seems dim, our finances, our relationships, our businesses because there is a WAR. There is always opposition.

Hannah's opponents were (1) herself; (2) Elkanah (husband); (3) Peninnah and her children. Observation tells us that Hannah:

1. **Herself,** warred with emotional distress and feelings of being a failure. Then feeling unworthy, she was described as feeling downhearted. Finally, Hannah was discouraged, ashamed, and depressed.
2. **Elkanah** (husband), Hannah warred with her relationship with her husband, Elkanah. At the same time, she knew that he loved her as he expressed his love and gave her a double portion of meat on the days of the sacrifice yearly. However, Hannah had a problem: He had children with Peninnah, and her womb was closed by the Lord.
3. "Now, her rival who provoked her sore to make her miserable to the point she did not eat." **Peninnah** was described as Hannah's adversary. We all have one. If you don't know his name, it is Devil. You can look Him up in **1st Peter 5:8, "Be sober, be vigilant because your adversary the devil, as a roaring lion, walketh about, seeking whom he may devour."**

Are you ready for the War?

I interpreted through observation that Hannah was ready for **WAR.** Her opponents, like man, focused on her outward appearance, but thanks be to God, he looks on the inward part, for he looks on the heart. In Ephesians 6:12, Paul wrote, "For we wrestle not against flesh and blood, but against principalities, against powers, against the rulers of the darkness of this world, against spiritual wickedness in high places."

Are you ready for the war? Let's check our artillery. Do you have the whole armor of God that ye may be able to stand against the wiles of the devil?

The **Holy Ghost,** I have it, according to *Acts 2nd chapter, fire baptized through the application of the name of Jesus. I've been submerged.* "Stand therefore, having your *loins girt about with*

truth, and ***having on the breastplate of righteousness;*** And your feet shod with the preparation of the gospel of peace; Above all, taking the ***shield of faith,*** wherewith ye shall be able to quench all the fiery darts of the wicked. And take the ***helmet of salvation,*** and the ***sword of the Spirit,*** which is the word of God."

I Declare WAR. **James 5:16** states, The effectual fervent prayer of the righteous man availeth much.

In the midst of oppression, persecution, and agony, Hannah found the strength and the ability to **Ignite**. Beat up, grief-stricken, disgusted, confused, hurt, ashamed, and barren, she found the strength to **fight**. Fight past being barren. Fight past opposition/disappointment. Fight past adversity. Failure is not an option. I will not take NO for an answer. I will take another route. Angry with good reason, in bitterness of soul and misjudgment of character, Hannah went to **WAR** in the Spirit. She applied what she knew. Hannah kept her vow to the Lord and gave Samuel as a servant for the rest of his days, never allowing a razor to come upon his head. She further praised and thanked God through a prayer of thanks. This walk of faith in God requires that we constantly check our artillery, for our weapons of this warfare are not carnal but mighty through God who prepares us for WAR. Remember that **Adversity Builds Character.**

7

THE POWER OF HOPE

I'm Calling *on MY Hope Hebrew 12:1-2:*

Wherefore, seeing we also are compassed about with so great a cloud of witnesses, let us lay aside every weight, and the sin which doth so easily beset us, and let us run with patience the race that is set before us, looking unto Jesus the author and finisher of our faith; who for the joy that was set before Him endured the cross, despising the shame, and is sat down at the right hand of the throne of God.

1st Peter 1:3-9, Peter wrote to encourage the suffering Christians. He wrote unto the strangers scattered. These Christians faced trials and persecution under Emperor Nero, hunted and killed throughout the Roman Empire.

Blessed be the God and Father of our Lord
Jesus Christ, which according to his
abundant mercy hath begotten us again

unto a lively hope by the resurrection of
Jesus Christ from the dead,

To an inheritance incorruptible, and
undefiled, and that fadeth not away,
reserved in heaven for you,

Who are kept by the power of God through
faith unto salvation ready to be revealed in
the last time.

Wherein ye greatly rejoice, though now for a
season, if need be, ye are in heaviness
through manifold temptations: That the
trial of your faith, being much more
precious than of gold that perisheth,
though it be tried with fire, might be found
unto praise and honour and glory at the
appearing of Jesus Christ:

Whom having not seen, ye love; in whom,
though now ye see Him not, yet believing,
ye rejoice with joy unspeakable and full of
glory: Receiving the end of your faith, even
the salvation of your souls.

Keys: *Begotten us again lively hope (Rebirth) kept by the Power of God through FAITH,* the Old English, Middle English, Greek, Hebrew word **Hope** and its many facets of meaning and phases of use. Peter refers to the Church as Living Stones (temple) and Christ as that Cornerstone, the foundation (1PETER 2:4-6) *To whom coming, as unto a living stone, disallowed indeed of men, but chosen of God, and precious, Ye also, as lively stones, are built up a spiritual house, a holy priesthood, to offer up spiritual sacrifices, acceptable to God by Jesus Christ. Wherefore also it is contained in the scripture, Behold, I lay in Zion a chief corner stone, elect, precious: and he that believeth on Him shall not be confounded.*

My hope! My faith! My belief! My trust! Hope has been defined as something that is hoped for. To believe, desire, trust, and expectation of fulfillment. Born with a measure. We understand hope as Now Faith, the substance of things hoped for and the evidence of things not seen, in accordance with Hebrews 11:1. The belief point begins with the belief in God's character, that He is who He says He is, and ending with the point that God will fulfill His promises even in the midst of not yet seeing the promises materializing (happen when we want them to). We are still to walk, act, and talk in FAITH, believing that Hope will bring you out because Hope answers. Hope is yet alive.

FAITH, "For Jesus said to Thomas, because thou hast seen me, thou hast believed: blessed are they that have not seen, and yet believed" (John 20:29). We find that Thomas doubted who Jesus was, that he had RISEN, and he wanted physiological (physical, tangible) proof that Jesus was who He said He was. The blessing for Thomas and many is that at times of doubt, there is a window and opportunity for belief. Because doubt leads to questions, and questions lead to answers, and when the answers become accepted, that DOUBT that you had has done a good work, because then doubt has deepened your faith. As you continue to search for answers, You DIG DEEPER.

> *For without controversy, great are the mysteries of Godliness, 1st. Timothy 3:16. "For my thoughts are not your thoughts neither are my ways your ways, saith the Lord. For as the heavens are higher than the earth, so are my ways higher than your ways, and my thoughts than your thoughts.*

> — ISAIAH 55:8-9

What is this HOPE? Who is this HOPE, and why do we have hope? Where is this hope? How does HOPE have POWER? What is Power? Understanding part of the definition of Hope can be a person or thing in which expectations are centered. Therefore, hope is built on the person or thing that has POWER, defined as the ability to do or act, capability of doing or accomplishing something. There are foundational premises. Someone is STANDING in the GAP. What is the GAP? The difference between what is and what is to come. The Gap recognizes a need.

Because God could find no man to stand in the GAP even after he looked and searched, according to the prophet Ezekiel 22:30, **he found no man to make up the hedge as to hold up the wall and to stand in the GAP to lead the people back to God,** so God who is a Spirit with all Power and Dominion, took matters into his own hands and prepared Himself a body, a physical state of **HOPE,** *not born of blood, nor of the will of the flesh, nor of the will of man, but of God (John 1:13-14). And the Word was made flesh and dwelt among us, (and we beheld his glory, the glory as of the only begotten of the Father), full of grace and truth. For, in the beginning was the Word and the Word was with God, and the Word was God. The same was in the beginning with God. All things were made by Him; and without Him was not anything made that was. In Him was life; and life was the light of men. Now we have POWER.*

Therefore, hope is Power, and Power is hope. These two are one. To sum them all up, my hope is **Jesus** (The Son of God), who is God manifested in the flesh, who holds all Power. No man comes to the Father except by Hope, and that Hope is Jesus. There is Power in Hope. That Hope is Jesus. *"Calling upon the name of Jesus, Ye shall receive Power after the Holy Ghost has come upon you," (Acts 1:8 power).* I AM Hope because I have Power, the Holy Ghost, which gives me Power. The Holy Ghost is on the inside of me, and it is roaring like a Lion. I am calling on My Hope, and the Power of my Hope is Jesus, my lively Hope, my Redeemer, the Chief Cornerstone/Foundation. My Hope is eternal. He springs from everlasting to everlasting; there is no end.

Jesus asked a question?

> *And Jesus went out, and his disciples, into the towns of Caesarea Philippi: and by the way he asked his disciples, saying unto them, Whom do men say that I am? And they answered, John the Baptist; but some say, Elias; and others, One of the prophets. And he saith unto them, But whom say ye that I am? And Peter answereth and saith unto Him, Thou art the Christ. And he charged them that they should tell no man of Him. And he began to teach them, that the Son of man must suffer many things, and be rejected of the elders, and of the chief priests, and scribes, and be killed, and after three days rise again*
>
> — MATTHEW 8:27

(Keep Hope Alive).

Rising with all Power, that lively stone, my Hope, went to prepare an eternal inheritance, a place called Heaven where ye may also be, but only if you believe. For those not defiled, not corrupted, those that have been kept by the Power of God. who is it that you say he is? If I adopt Prophet Isaiah 53:5, as I had, to call on my Hope who ministered to me, and I made this personal in the midst of my trials, I know the Power of God is keeping me.

Make this personal: "For He was wounded for my transgressions, he was bruised for my iniquities, the chastisement of my peace was upon Him and by his stripes I AM healed." I AM made whole. Hope will bring Me out!

Things to Remember!

The Power of Hope lays hands on the sick and watches them recover! The Power of Hope delivered Moses and the children of Israel from bondage through the Exodus, the coming out! Daniel called on that Hope in the Lion's Den! The Power of Hope freed Paul and Silas from jail! The Power of Hope Answered by Fire! The Power of Hope rained down Manna from on high!

Will you call on your Hope? I'm calling on My Hope in the name of Jesus.

_____

_____

_____

_____

_____

_____

_____

_____

_____

_____

_____

_____

_____

_____

_____

_____

_____

_____

_____

_____

_____

_____

8

JOURNEY OF A DREAMER
(FOCUSED DREAMER WITH NO EXCUSES)

A Journey defined as the act of traveling from one place to another, especially when involving a considerable distance; a trip; A process or course likened to traveling signifying a beginning or the process of something in effort to get somewhere at some appointed time.

The plan of salvation is a journey, a journey of life. We all have them. This walk of life is an experience of a journey, a compilation of journeys exemplified by winding roads, hills, mountains, pain, agony, problems, issues, circumstances, storms, and rain within our lives. It began on our date of birth, but the expected time after the dash in the middle is unknown to us all.

The Bible makes note that life is like a **VAPOUR**. According to *James 4:14, "Whereas ye know not what shall be on the morrow. For what is your life? It is even a vapour, that appeareth for a little time, and then vanisheth away."*

A vapor - a substance diffused or suspended in the air,

especially one normally liquid or solid. When we understand the true essence of our life expectancy, then and only then can we navigate through our journey with an essence of importance, urgency, and awareness of the FACTOR of TIME; the cliché **"TIME is of the ESSENCE."** Time is valuable and precious and cannot be replaced if **WASTED.** I will not waste my time. Stop Wasting Invaluable Time Contemplating Hindrance. It is time to SWITCH from invaluable behaviors and focus your thoughts to accomplish things as a dreamer.

Dreamer: (1.) a person who dreams; (2.) a person who lives in a world of fantasy; one who is impractical and unrealistic; (3.) a person whose ideas or projects are considered: *audacious; or highly speculative; visionary.*

The Journey of a dreamer is audacious *(extremely bold or daring; recklessly brave; fearless, visionary,)* meaning envisioned, seeing it before it happens.

For without a vision, what happens to the Church?

Proverbs 29:18, Solomon writes, "Where there is no vision, the people perish: but he that keepeth the law, happy is he." With a Vision - the act or power of anticipating that which will or may come to be: a revelation that is received by prophets, but knowledge of God is required. Wisdom is a need. *Proverbs 1:7, "The fear of the Lord is the beginning of knowledge: but fools despise wisdom and instruction."*

A vision should ignite within others and empower them to rise, for we understand in the Beginning, God, who created all things, the heavens, and the earth in the fullness, had dreams, a vision for the Church, being us, who was on the inside of Him. God had goals and aspirations "for MANKIND." However, on this journey, man SINNED, placing enmity and separation between man and God. But GOD, the Author and the Finisher of our FAITH, stayed on the Journey of a Dreamer, the Journey of a Visionary, a leader, a Redeemer, that the Church will not perish but live and live more abundantly. While having to alter his plans, He never stopped dreaming, He never stopped being in existence, and He never stopped the Journey. Just because our plans are altered does not mean we stop our journey or that we stop dreaming, but that we learn to assimilate into whatever plan God has for us with an understanding that He will accommodate all of our needs, for He is our Shepherd. He will navigate us through all our valleys, for the Lord is your Shepherd, you shall not want.

Ecclesiastes 3:1 tells us, "To everything, there is a season and a time to every Purpose under the heavens." It might not be your time right now but stay on the Journey. It may not be your season right now but keep dreaming. You may still be seeking your purpose. Stay on the Journey of a Dreamer, for in due season, **you will reap if you Faint Not!**

Are you yet dreaming?

_____

_____

_____

_____

_____

_____

_____

_____

_____

_____

_____

_____

_____

_____

_____

_____

_____

_____

9

FRAGMENTED MIND

2 Timothy 1:7 For God hath not given us the spirit of fear; but of power, and of love, and of a sound mind. (Paul, from jail writing, is giving instructions and encouraging Timothy, a young Pastor of the church at Ephesus during a time of great opposition for believers and non-believers).

If there be therefore any consolation in Christ, if any comfort of love, if any fellowship of the Spirit, if any bowels and mercies, Fulfil ye my joy, that ye be likeminded, having the same love, being of one accord, of one mind. Let nothing be done through strife or vain glory; but in lowliness of mind let each esteem other better than themselves. Look not every man on his own things, but every man also on the things of others. Let this mind be in you, which was also in Christ Jesus: (Paul from jail to Philippians to strengthen them that they might understand that true Joy only comes from Christ.

— PHILIPPIANS 2:1-5

*S*ound Mind or /sṓphrōn, defined as: of sound mind, self-controlled, temperate, sober-minded, modest, chaste. "Acting in God's definition of balance." In English, sound mind means sane or rational. The state of one's mind is adequate with the ability to reason, to think, to process thoughts and emotions. In some way, man gets away from the scripture as it relates to a **Sound Mind.** In some way, we find ourselves Spiritually Drifting, going away from our first love, disrupting the balance that God has placed in our lives.

Understand that there are some medical causes, such as mental health disorders. Examples include depression, bipolar disorder, schizophrenia, substance abuse, brain injury, dementia, seizure disorders, or conditions of extreme sleep deprivation or isolation, to name a few. These include but are not limited to sin, people, places, things, church hurt, backbiting, frustration, fear, stress, money, lack of or activation of power, death, imprisonment, persecution, and being counted out. The list can go on and on.

Bondage is a state of mind.

But Paul asked a question in (Romans 8:35) and answered in Romans 8:36-39 and Romans 8:36-39.

> *Who shall separate us from the love of Christ? shall tribulation, or distress, or persecution, or famine, or nakedness, or peril, or sword?*
> *As it is written, for thy sake we are killed all the day long; we are accounted as sheep for the slaughter.*
> *Nay, in all these things we are more than*

> *conquerors through Him that loved us.*
> *For I am persuaded, that neither death, nor life, nor*
> *angels, nor principalities, nor powers, nor*
> *things present, nor things to come,*
> *Nor height, nor depth, nor any other creature, shall*
> *be able to separate us from the love of God,*
> *which is in Christ Jesus our Lord.*

Fragments: A noun defined as a small part broken or separated off something. An isolated or incomplete part of something. In a verb, Fragments is defined as "a break or cause to break into fragments or something breaking into pieces." The one thing about a fragment of something is that we know it was once a part of a **Whole.** It belonged to something; it was a part of something. You are or once were a part of the **PACT, the Body of Christ. Stay with the Pact. Fragments of the mind symptomize ISOLATION leaving you as Prey for the Adversary. So be sober, be vigilant, for your enemy (adversary, the devil) is like a roaring lion walking to and forth seeking whom he may devour. (1st Peter 5:8). Seeking to steal your joy, kill your spirit and to destroy your relationship with God.**

The **Mind,** referred to as a noun, is defined as a person's intellect. The element of a person that enables them to be aware of the world and their experiences, to think, and to feel; the faculty of consciousness and thought. Psychologists refer to the mind as the **totality of conscience and unconscious mental processes and activities.** We often use the cliché "A Mind is a Terrible Thing to Waste." When we think about **Fragments** of a Mind. The study of human behavior tells us there has been a break in the mind's or (psyche's) normal way of functioning. Psychologists refer to this as a psychotic break. There has been an acute – a short period of time, an interruption - primary psychosis.

You have gotten **out of touch with reality.** You can no longer tell what is real and what is not. I believe it was The Ghetto Boys who said, "My Mind is Playing Tricks on Me." I have gotten out of sorts with reality. "What is really going on?" This break in the conscious. This break in the intellect, in my will, in my sensibility leaves the mind fragmented, distorted, seeking to become whole again, with a longing to become whole again, a thirst after righteousness. **"Blessed are those who hunger and thirst for righteousness, for they shall be filled,"** (Matthew 5:6).

Lyrics of Mary Mary in their hit record Take the Shackles of My Feet So I Can Dance says, **"In the corners (fragments) of mind, I just can't seem to find a reason to believe that I can break free 'cause you see I have been down for so long, feel like the hope is gone, but as I lift my hands, I understand that I should praise you through my circumstance."**

Fragmented Mind, it is time to break free. It is time to take back what the enemy has stolen, distorted, or disturbed. It is time to break free from that false sense and pretense of reality that the enemy has placed in your mind, for you can only serve One Master, One Faith, One Lord, One Baptism. **"A double-minded man is unstable in all of his ways"** (James 1:8).

How do I get free? How do I get Free? How do I get back to "Acting in the Balance of God?" The time is **Now!** (Now Faith). Time to allow our circumstances to *NO* longer negatively dictate our relationship with God. To No longer drive us away from God but to push us to God.

The Song says, **The Word, The Word of God, brought me Out. The Word changed my way of Thinking.**

(Isaiah 53:5) For He was wounded for my transgressions he was bruised for my iniquities the chastisement of my peace was upon Him and by his stripes I am healed. I am made whole, fragmented mind breaking free.

David said *(Psalm 51:10) Create in me a clean heart, O God; and renew a right spirit within me... break free.*

Paul said *(Romans 12:1-2) I beseech you therefore brethren by the mercies of God that you present your body as a living sacrifice Holy and Acceptable unto God which is your reasonable service. And be not conformed to this world: but ye transformed by the renewing of your mind, that ye may prove what is good and the perfect will of God break free.*

James said *(4:7-10)* King James Version (KJV)*Submit yourselves therefore to God. Resist the devil, and he will flee from you. Draw nigh to God, and he will draw nigh to you. Cleanse your hands, ye sinners; and purify your hearts, ye double minded break free. Be afflicted, and mourn, and weep: let your laughter be turned to mourning, and your joy to heaviness. Humble yourselves in the sight of the Lord, and he shall lift you up break free.*

Paul said to Timothy, so I say to you in *(Philippians 2:5) Let this mind be in you that was also, in Christ Jesus... Therefore, we must humble ourselves having the mind of Christ.* Remember that Lively Hope that is on the inside of you roaring like a lion; let it ROAR. It is time for you to break free right in the midst of your circumstances, breaking free into the Joy of the Lord. So I'll lean to the Lord's understanding and Break Free.

And Moses said unto the Lord, O my Lord, I am not eloquent, neither heretofore, nor since thou hast spoken unto thy servant: but I am slow of speech, and of a slow tongue. And the Lord said unto Him, Who hath made man's mouth? Or who maketh the dumb, or deaf, or the seeing, or the blind? Have not I the Lord? Now therefore go, and I will be with thy mouth, and teach thee what thou shalt say.

— EXODUS 4:10-12

10

SPEAK THE WORD

There is something about fluent and effective communication. There is nothing like good conversation. Open dialogue, for some, is used as an outward expression of their inner thoughts, feelings, emotions, and opinions or the means to which they get their point across.

For some, they get you told. It is a method for some to resolve problems/conflicts to hold, to gain, or give attention to. Some individuals open their mouths and immediately command attention, captivating their populated audience and gaining full control of the environment in which they are speaking. We find at the beginning of the conception of time, God spoke the Word, and things began to happen, for God said let there be, and there was. We see that God opened his mouth and commanded the attention of this once dark and voided environment and spoke the beginning into existence, the institution of time.

We understand to speak means to utter words or articulate

sounds with the ordinary voice, talk, communicate vocally; mention, converse, deliver an address, discourse, et cetera; to make a statement in written or printed words.

You must be willing to open your mouth! There is a difference between praising God as an emotional response to his goodness as opposed to an act of the will. David said, **"I will bless the Lord at all times and his praises shall continually be in my mouth." (Psalm 34:1).** We understand that the *"Power of Life and Death Lies in the tongue, and they that love it shall eat the fruit thereof" (Proverbs 18:21)* Learn to effectively use your Words! Your words - this combination of letters, speech, or talk expresses one's emotion in words. Words are Powerful!

Something happens when you begin to speak those things. Something happens when you begin to speak the Word: **"In the beginning was the Word, and the Word was with God, and the Word was God" (John 1:1).** There is Power in the Word.

The Word of God is what brought me out. The engrafted Word, that implanted Word, is down on the inside of me (James 1:21), telling me to go ahead.

David said, "Thou word have I hid in my heart that I might not sin against thee" (Psalm 119:11). Speak the Word, *"For it is written man shall not live by bread alone, but by every word that proceedeth out of the mouth of God" (Matthew 4:4).* Speak the Word, *"For our weapon of this warfare is not carnal but mighty through God to the pulling down of strongholds" (2nd Corinthians 10:4).* I am Speaking the Word, *"The sword of the spirit the word of God it is my weapon of choice (Ephesians 6:17).*

I will speak the Word in the midst of it. I will speak the Word. The Word changes situations. The Word opens doors. The Word brings about change. The Word causes things to happen. The Word makes ways for existence. The word made a way for my escape. The Word changes atmospheres. The Word brings deliverance. The Word brings praises. The Word brings conviction. The Word heals. The Word gets you in the presence of God. The Word loses shackles. Will you speak the Word? The word said, "No Weapon formed against you shall prosper." The Word said, "Touch not my anointed and do my prophet no harm." The Word said, "Greater that is within me than he that is in the world."

Will You? Speak the Word!

_____

_____

_____

_____

_____

_____

_____

_____

_____

_____

_____

_____

_____

_____

_____

_____

_____

_____

_____

_____

_____

_____

_____

_____

_____

_____

_____

11

GOD WILL MAKE A WAY

Luke 22:39-46 (Jesus's Agony in the Garden) Saying, Father, if thou be willing, remove this cup from me: nevertheless, not my Will, but thou Will, be done.

2nd Timothy 2:16-17, Paul's charge to Timothy, this young leader. The Bible, God's inspired Word, God-Breathed, written by inspiration of the Holy Spirit. We learn to observe, interpret, and apply to our lives. Learning his Will? How? The Plan of Salvation, Purpose to learn to do his Will to help others.

This writing is meant to solely focus on yourself as an individual, inwardly speaking, critically internalizing, thinking beyond the veil, beyond the surface of what you see, feel, or hear. Both consciously and conscientiously meditating on the thoughts of one's own journey. How did I get here? Pointing to yourself, state, **"This one is personal. This one is just for me."**

The "Here" meaning where you are in the NOW. "Now unto Him that is able to keep me" routes, we all have them: some came from the south, north, east, and west. Some were forced, lost, called, chosen, willing, curious, tired, beat up, hurt, scared, sick, addicted, bankrupt, whatever the route. We all have a navigation system in common: *That pillar in a cloud by day and that pillar of Fire by Night.* (Ex. 13:21); the song says, "doesn't matter how you get here, just get here if you can," **For I Am the way, the truth, and the life. No man comes to the Father except by me. (John 14:6)**

Our journey in life many times would be different if we forever prayed, forever found ourselves in one-on-one harmony with God, that "Effectual Prayer," that "Fervent Prayer," seeking and adhering to God in prayer. I say this because often, individuals do not pray for various reasons. But on this topic **focus,** some do not pray because there is a lack of belief that anything is being done or that anything is happening, **but do you know that with God, something is always happening?** God is always working (Romans 8:21). *"And being fully persuaded that, what he had promised, he was able also to perform"* (Romans 4:21). Abraham never wavered in God's Promise, becoming a Father of many nations, remaining strong in faith, giving all Glory to God (Romans 4:20).

Nosily we are always trying to figure out when God is going to work. We do not see movement, so we begin to panic and to ask questions like, when is God going to do it when the fact of the matter is that God is always working it out for your good. The song says, "I don't know how, I don't know when, but I know He's going to do it!" God is always working. He is always working it out for you.

God is a spirit. God just IS. God is just Being. If we paused here, have you ever been linked into the spirit of God that you just BE in God, I'm just being at Peace. I just want to Be Happy, Be in Existence. God Who Is, God the I AM, this supreme power having all dominion. **God from Teman (Habakkuk 3:3),** the deliverer of Israel's children, the Great Exodus, the Coming Out. God hears his children praying for deliverance after **400** years (Genesis 15:13) of oppression. God heard, saw, and knew their sorrows and came down to deliver them by way of Moses. (Ex. 3:6-8) God Will! It was His Will that they come out; it is His will that you come out and be delivered, and you must will to let it happen.

Will: Wish, purpose, desire, or intellect; what God wills, purposes or desires.

What is God's will? His will and His wish for us is stated plainly: *"Above all things it is that I Prosper and be in Good health that my soul also prospers"* (3 John 2). God will make a way, *for I know the thoughts I think towards you, saith the Lord, thoughts of peace and not evil, to give to you an expected end" (Jeremiah 29:11).* It will not always be like this! God will make a way!

Take a good look at me. It will not always be like this! Always working, God is either answering the way you have hoped (Now Faith) or changing your heart by spiritual intercession to bring your prayer into harmony with his will. **Luke 22:42, "Not my will, but Thine will be done."** Prayer unanswered, so you thought. Isaiah 59:1-2 says, Behold, the Lord's hand is not shortened, that it cannot save; neither his ear heavy that it cannot hear:

Something happened.

> But your iniquities have separated between you
> and your God, and your sins have hid his
> face from you, that he will not hear.

> — *ISAIAH 59:2*

Make this personal: Let's get back in His WILL - Can you say, "But God is changing me; he is working on me; I am learning to know that the prayer unanswered keeps me in his Will.

"Let this mind be in me that was also, in Christ Jesus" (Paul

Philippians 2:5), understanding that God will make a way!

Cleanse me from my sin O God. Create in me a Clean Heart, renew a Right Spirit within me (David Psalm 51). God Will Make a Way. "And we know that all things work together for good to them that love God, to them who are the called according to his purpose" (Romans 8:28). Everything is working for my Good. The hurt I experienced is working my good.

God Will Make a Way!

_____
_____
_____
_____
_____
_____
_____
_____
_____
_____
_____
_____
_____
_____
_____
_____
_____
_____
_____
_____
_____
_____
_____

12

FIGHT! FIGHT! STAY IN THE FIGHT!

There is a proverb that says, "In the fear of the Lord there is strong confidence"

— *PROVERBS 14:16*

---

*O*ften, we need reassurance. We need encouragement. We need a reminder of where our help lies and our strength comes from. Well, the psalmist says, *"I will lift my eyes unto the hills, from whence cometh all my help" My help cometh from the Lord, which made the heaven and the earth"* (Psalm 121:1-2). Nehemiah (8:10) said, "for the joy of the Lord is your strength." David said: The Lord is my strength and my shield: my heart trusted in Him, and I am helped: therefore, my heart greatly rejoiceth: and my song will I praise Him. **"The Lord is their strength, and he is the saving strength of his anointed" (Psalm 28:6-7). Touch not my anointed and do my prophet no harm"** (1st Chronicles 16:22). Paul says in (2nd Timothy 2:19): "Nevertheless the foundation of God standeth sure, having this seal, The Lord knoweth them that are his. And, let everyone that nameth the name of Christ depart from iniquity." "The name of the Lord is a strong tower: the righteous runneth into it and is safe" (Proverbs 8:10). "Who is this King of glory? The Lord strong and mighty, the "Lord mighty in battle." David goes on to say, "Lift up your heads," O ye gates: even lift them up, ye everlasting doors: and the King of glory shall come in." "Who is this King of glory? The Lord of hosts, he is the King of glory" Selah

Fight or Flight is the instinctive physiological response to a threatening situation that readies one either to resist forcibly or to run away. We understand that to fight means "to contend with, to engage in battle, to gain in the struggle." Flight means the act of fleeing, to run away, retreat. But we understand on the Lord's side that fleeing is not an option when you must STAND and SEE the SALVATION of the Lord. We see God told Saul, the appointed king of the children of Israel, to go smite (attack) Amalek, and utterly destroy all that they have, and spare them not, but slay both man and woman, infant and suckling, ox and sheep, camel and ass. This is a War, Y'all! It is time to Stand UP. *Obedience to God is better than sacrifice* (1st Sam 15:22). Observe, interpret and apply the point to yourself. In 1st Samuel 15:18, Samuel says to Paul, *"And the Lord sent thee on a journey, and said, Go and utterly destroy the sinners the Amalekites, and FIGHT against them until they are consumed."* God said FIGHT against them, don't run, don't hide, do not turn a deaf ear, do not partially disobey Him. He said FIGHT, for we are fighting against SIN and all UNRIGHTEOUSNESS. **For the wages of SIN is death but the gift of God is eternal life** (Romans 6:23).

"FIGHT! FIGHT! STAY IN THE FIGHT." "Put on the whole armor they ye may be able to stand against the wiles of the devil. After you have done all you can, stand." *"For we wrestle (struggle, fight) not against flesh and blood, but against principalities, against powers, against the rulers of the darkness of this world, against spiritual wickedness in high places"* (Epeshians.6:12).

"Finally, my brethren, be strong in the Lord and in the Power of his might" (Ephesians 6:10). You must stay in the fight. 1st Corinthians 9:26-27, "I therefore so run, not as uncertainly; so, fight I, not as one that beateth the air. But I keep under my body, and bring it into subjection, lest that by any means when I have preached to others, I myself should be a castaway."

"Stay in The Fight."

> *I therefore so run, not as uncertainly; so fight I, not as one that beateth the air:*
>
> — 1ST CORINTHIANS 9:26

If I Can Go the Distance, I Shall Wear a Crown

Distance: The extent or amount of space between two things, points, lines, or the full length of a race. How hard you can get hit and keep moving forward? How much can you take and keep moving forward? That is how winning is done! (Rocky IV)

STAY IN THE FIGHT

Genesis 12:1-8
Hebrews 11:8-10 - Great Heroes
Deuteronomy 1:1-4

_____

_____

_____

13

WHEN GOD SAYS MOVE

MOVE BY FAITH!

Oftentimes in life, we as individuals like to map out our own plans, as if we are the ones in control of our own destiny, our (spiritual) life journey.

a s the children of Israel, we know it took them 40, almost a 41-year detour because of disobedience. o years, eleven months, and one month, in mourning, for Moses to be exact, before entering the Promised Land, which was an eleven-day journey, and getting off track, forgetting who the Author and the Finisher of their Faith is. For we find in Hebrews 12:2, "*Looking unto Jesus, the Author and Finisher of our faith; who for the joy that was set before Him endured the cross, despising the shame, and has sat down at the right hand of the throne of God.*" Before this reward is obtained, we find that there were instructions, at least three given, that Jesus followed. First, in verse 12:1, "Wherefore seeing we also are compassed about with so great a cloud of witnesses."

1. You are not alone. Let us lay aside every weight that so easily beset us,

2. Put down, give up whatever endangers your relationship with God, and let us run with patience the race that is set before us,

3. Run, move forward for Christ, not ourselves. This race is not given to the swift nor to the strong, but to the one that endureth to the end (Ecclesiastes 9:11).

The word *"Let" is* defined as not prevent or forbid; allow. Understanding that "Let" is a synonym meaning to allow, authorize, giving a command that one must follow. We found, in the beginning, that God said, *"Let us make man in our own image"* (Genesis 1:26-28), and Man came forth by the command of God. (When God says Move, Move)

Move means "To go in a specified direction or manner or change position." When you move, you show progression. We understand that God is a progressive God. He is always moving. He is not standing still, nor is He idle. He is forever performing miracle after miracle. *For God is a Spirit and those that worship Him must worship Him in spirit and in truth (John 4:24).*

To worship Him, you must first believe that God is, by FAITH, and that he is a rewarder of them that diligently seek Him (Hebrews 11:6), for, without FAITH, it is impossible to please God. For FAITH is - The substance of things hoped for the evidence of things not seen (Hebrews 11:1).

By Faith, I move when God says move! This leads to an intimate relationship with God. Of course, we desire intimacy among ourselves with others, but what about intimacy with God, the Author and Creator of intimacy? Without questions, we dance to the beat of everyone else's drum. What about dancing to the beat of the Lord?

The anonymous author of Psalm 150 writes, "Praise ye the Lord. Praise God in his sanctuary. Praise Him in the firmament of his power. Praise Him for his mighty acts. Praise Him according to his excellent greatness. Praise Him with the sound of the trumpet. Praise Him with the psaltery and harp. Praise Him with the tumbrel and dance. Praise Him with stringed instruments and/or organs. Praise Him upon the loud cymbals. Praise Him upon the high-sounding cymbals. Let everything that hath breath praise the Lord. Praise ye the Lord."

When God said "Move," Abraham moved and positioned Himself to receive the promise.

Genesis 2:15-17 (18 -23 Woman) 3:1-6 (Problem SIN-Disobedience by deception)- Moses

Isaiah 53: 5-7,10-12 (Resolution to Problem, Problem Solved Reconciliation) - Isaiah Call Back Philippians 2: verse 2 Verses 5-11 (My Rights) - Paul taught the Philippians to show that true joy comes from Jesus.

_____

_____

_____

_____

_____

_____

_____

_____

_____

_____

_____

_____

_____

_____

_____

_____

_____

14

WE HAD A PROBLEM, BUT I GOT IT RIGHT!

We had a problem - any question or matter involving doubt, uncertainty, or difficulty; a question proposed for solution or discussion.

---

*B*ut I Got A Right - Correct or morally proper; righteous in accord with justice to become justified in an intimate relationship with God.

Social Policies are constructed because a problem is classified as a social problem. Social problems do not just exist but are constructed. *For starters, social problems are (1) identified/chosen; (2) framed or defining it (SIN); and (3) offering an explanatory theory giving social policy a purpose to help people improve the qualities of their lives.* With that in mind, social policy also restrains, contains, controls, and suppresses people. When identifying a problem out of the many there are, we understand that there is a problem with one's quality of life. Social policies are created to solve the identified problems through awareness and advocacy on a political, social, and economical platform.

We find in Genesis, the second and third chapters, a problem. If we redefine the problem, we will classify the problem as SIN by deception, leading to disobedience and causing a separation **between God and Man.**

If I never had a problem, I would not know that God could solve them. I'd never know He could answer prayer, that He could answer by fire, that He could deliver me. If I had never had a problem I identified, I would never know who God IS.

We find out that the tension of some unmet needs, poverty, lack of health care, civil rights, and minimum wage leads to a definition by social movements to address the problem. Understand that social policies are just one level of public policies. But public policy is defined as the system of laws, measurements, courses of action, and funding priorities funded by a governmental entity or its representatives. We understand that these identified problems led to movements and the Bill of Rights to rectify the identified problems. Nowadays, everyone and everything has rights, but what about the Apostles' movement and the redemption of Man? Let's talk about the movement of the righteous, or how about the movement of God? What About the movement of the Holy Ghost?

Well, having the movement of Jesus, having the mind of Christ, I have a right to lift Him up, to give God praise, for He solves all my problems and supplies all my needs according to His riches in Glory! I have the right to tell Him, "Thank You!" I have a right to send up Judah, for He is worthy of my praise. He's due honor in my worship! I have a right! On Calvary, He gave me the right! O, I believe. I've confessed with my mouth. I've tarried. I've received the Holy Ghost Power. I've gone down in the name of Jesus and came up in the newness of life. I got a right!

The world did not give it to me, and the world can't take it away! God gave me the right through Christ Jesus to serve Him, praise, and worship Him in spirit and truth. My worship is for real! I've got a right to lift Him higher, to praise Him harder. O, I got a right! You cannot hinder, stop, or block me because I got a right.

I got a right to enter His gates with thanksgiving and His courts with praise! I got a right to praise Him on the stringed instruments, on the high-sounding cymbals. So let everything that hath breath praise ye the Lord for He is worthy! He is worthy. He is worthy to be praised. He is highly lifted up!

You have been served. You just got your notification! This is my response: My problems are not greater than my praise! God did that, and I got a right! Smile, for He inhabits the praises of His people! Smile on my life, O God, for you gave me the Right! I am grateful you did not leave me, O God, in my sin, iniquities, or transgression, but you gave me another chance. You solved the problem, took hold of sin, took them all the way to the cross, and left them there! God, I thank you for the right! Lord, I thank you for the right! Thank you, Jesus. Thank Jesus for the Right!

Problem solved. I've got a Right! Wherever I go, I've got a right to tell Him, "Thank You!" I've got a right! I count it a privilege. It is an honor to magnify You, to lift You up from the fruit my lips, the depths of my heart. I got a Right! O that men would praise Me. O that men would lift Me up! Higher! Higher! I would draw all men unto me. I have a right!

In the good times, in the bad times, and in-between times, I have the right. I have an obligation, a debt I could never pay.

I Have a Right

_____

_____

_____

_____

_____

_____

_____

_____

_____

_____

_____

_____

_____

_____

_____

_____

_____

_____

_____

_____

_____

_____

_____

_____

_____

_____

_____

_____

15

OUT OF THE SHADOW OF MAN

(WOMEN, WE ARE STRONG)

Women, We Are Strong. "Favour is deceitful and beauty is vain, but a woman that feareth the Lord, she shall be praised."

— *PROVERBS 31:30*

"Out of the Shadow of Man." How befitting to *"Women we are Strong," Proverbs 31:30.* "Out of the Shadow of Man," and "Women, we are Strong." These composites of a woman in this proverb represent Strength. Strong: Having morals, strength, and courage. Truly, these should be aspirations of us all.

We understand that often we as individuals fall short in the areas of "Being True to Who We Are," quite often seeking to form the identity of others upon ourselves because of our own insecurities instead of embracing the *"fearfully and wonderfully"* (Psalm 114:39) made creation God has created one uniquely to be. Many times coining the phrase "but if I could be like someone else," in essence, by way of example, "only if I had what such and such had, I'd," "if my hair was long like, if my complexion was not as dark like, if I had more full lips as such and such, if I was taller I could be like, If I could speak or praise like," but what happened to being happy with who you are and being more like Christ, just to be more like Jesus.

One thing I have recently learned is that to be more like Christ, there is a command for you to deny (give up) yourself and follow Christ. Part of this summons by invitation commands us to pick up our cross and follow Christ. Dare to mention there are things along the way we all must deny ourselves of, things for the love of Christ we must forsake. (Matthew 16:24). So, we will not always get what we want when we want or how we want it." For all things in God's will are "Yes." The question is, "Is it in His will"? *Many are the devices in a man's heart. Nevertheless, only the counsel of Lord shall stand." (Psalm19:21)*

We find that there are levels of discipline in naming the name of the Lord. Discipline requires strength, tenacity, resilience, and self-control to behave by way of obedience to the rules, guidelines, codes, and commandments of God. (Hebrew 12:14). *For we are to follow men with all peace and holiness without no man shall see the Lord.* Holiness is a standard, a disciplined way of living, a way of being and behaving, a thought process of mind, and a way of thinking that forbids leaning on your own understanding. Requesting that you *"Let this mind be in you that was also in Christ Jesus"* (Philippians 2:5). Having the mind of Christ, being in Christ, by the renewing of your mind, you have become a *new creature; old things are passed away and behold all things become new" (2nd Corinthians 5:17)* "Out of the Shadow of Man," Women, we are strong.

By definition, Shadow means, in this reference, "To follow (a person) about secretly to keep watch over his movements." Just by way of this in-particular definition of the word shadow, we automatically know if we have the mind of Christ; that our eyes and thoughts are not lining up with following Christ. We have people that have lived in the shadow of others for years and decades. Some have gone to their graves without stepping out of the shadow and into Faith, Now Faith, and being who God called them to be.

Thus, leaving room for the blame game, we understand that we all must be good followers before becoming great leaders. The first part of a disciple of Christ is being a pupil, a student, but there is a clause. "We follow man as they follow Christ." "Do not keep your eyes faceted upon individuals but keep your eyes on the move of God." For everything is moving by the Power of God. I live, breathe, and move. I have my being by the Power of God.

He said in his word that "a man's gift makes room for Him, and bringeth Him before great men," Proverbs 18:16. The more we start to understand to allow our light to also shine, the more strength we gain to come out of the shadow. The more we understand that your light cannot be hidden, the more resilient you become to bounce back from adversity. The more we overcome the wiles of the devil, the stronger we become to stand and see the salvation of the Lord. The more we cast our cares upon the Lord, the greater our praise. The more we understand that the *"Joy of the Lord is our strength"* (Nehemiah 8:10), the stronger we become, the brighter we shine. We no longer walk in shadows, but God is the light of our salvation who directs our *path as a lamp unto my feet and a light unto my path* (Psalm119:105). Out of the Shadow of Man, Women, we are Strong.

Lemuel asked a question in this proverb: "Who can find a virtuous woman? For her price is far above rubies." Who can find a woman (wife) (mother) of excellence that exudes strength, confidence, grace, and knows her net worth? This woman possesses many skills and is compassionate and submissive. This woman girds herself with strength. She prepares herself for action. This woman makes her arms strong; strength and dignity are her clothing. This woman opens her mouth and speaks wisdom. This woman understands *favor* is deceitful, and beauty is vain. Beauty will pass away, but she is a woman that feareth the Lord. She shall be praised. Let her work praise her in the gates. Who is this woman?

This is that woman who no longer hides in the shadows of others. This woman is secure in the woman God has called her to be. This woman is strong in the power of the Lord, this praying woman that stands boldly in the fear of the Lord. This woman of strength and wisdom builds her house up while the foolish women pluck hers down with her bare hands. This woman finds strength in the midst of those that criticized her for breaking her alabaster box of precious oil at the feet of our Savior (Luke 7:37-38). This woman who got in the press through the crowd to grab hold of her deliverance and her healing, this woman. The widow who gave 32 mites, giving all that she had (Luke 21). "Women, we are strong." This woman was impregnated with destiny and carried the Word for nine long months. She watched her son's crucifixion upon a cross. This woman of strength, this woman of valor, who is this woman? This woman that drew a male child from the water loved and nurtured Him as her very own, only for Him to lead the Exodus, "The Coming Out of Israel," who can find this woman? Let's not forget the five wise women who awaited the bridegroom's coming who packed extra olive oil, unlike the five foolish women who ran out of oil and had no light. The bridegroom came, for we must be ye also ready, for we don't know the day nor the hour of Jesus' return. (Matthew 25:1-13) Out of the Shadow of Man, Women, we are strong.

16

LORD, DON'T LET ME LOSE MY PASSION FOR YOU

FINISH WHAT YOU STARTED

(1 John 3:1-2, 11-24)

We know that often in life, in this walk, on this journey, we find ourselves getting off course. The study of spiritual drifting has shown itself in our personal space at one time or another. If you haven't experienced this, if I say it like my grandmother used to, Just Keep on Living. At times spiritual drifting causes us to complain, become bored, complacent, tired, and burned out, using statements like "I'm Over It" or whatever it is that we are doing or were once passionate about. Many have found that the Church, the Body of Christ, and the baptized believers' movement have experienced these thoughts, feelings, and emotions both spiritually and naturally. Keep in mind that the enemy comes to *"wear out the saints of the Most High God" (Daniel 7:25)*.

When we look at the word Passion, passion is "Any powerful or compelling emotion or feeling, as love or hate. A Strong amorous feeling or desire; love; ardor." Passion drives, pulls, pushes, or motivates an individual to act in some shape, form and/or fashion. We know that some people have married, had babies all because of passion; fought, killed because of passion; stalked because of passion; lied, cheated because of passion, went without because of passion; placed themselves and/or their children in harm's way because of passion, how about we have a **Savior** that gave His life all because of **Passion**. *God* sent forth his only begotten son all because of Passion. Love, that of the Agape, the love that is pure and unchangeable, doesn't faint or waver because of our circumstances or our shortcomings. Through it all, the love of God yet remains the same. Even when we choose to walk away, His love for us yet remains the same.

For *"Jesus Christ is the same yesterday today and forevermore" (Hebrew 13:8).* God requires us to *"let brotherly love continue" (Hebrew 13:1).* God Himself is love: *Commanding his love towards us in that, while we were yet sinners Christ died for us.* If we must talk about Passion (Romans 5:8). Let's talk about the Passion of Jesus Christ. For God So Loved the world that He gave (John 3:16).

He said in his word, *"Thou shalt love the Lord thy God with all thy heart, and with all thy soul, and with all thy mind. This is the first and great commandment. And the second is like unto it, Thou shalt love thy neighbor as thyself. On these two commandments hang all the law and the prophets" (Matthew 22:37-40).*

"If you want to see Jesus, you have to Love." Love, the *"Love (Charity) of Christ, covers a multitude of sin, causing you to be hospitable one to another without grudging" (1st Peter 4:7-8).* Therefore, understand that Love, that true love, passionate love, is an action word. It requires you to do something.

Religion. We know it is defined according to the scripture James 1:27, *"Pure religion and undefiled (pure) before God and the Father is this, to visit the Fatherless and widows in their affliction, and to keep Himself unspotted from the world."* So we understand God is calling us to be pure in everything that we do; with our whole heart to do everything that we do as we are doing it unto the Lord, that He may be gloried up in heaven that he may be pleased with our life, pleased with our works, our denials, and our sacrifices.

Lord, don't let me lose my passion for You. I've got to finish what I started. I do not want to just be a hearer, but a doer of your word, for faith without works is dead" (James 2:17). Lord, do not let me lose my "Savor." I want to yet be salty, of use for your Kingdom." I don't want my love to wax cold. I want to be the "Change Agent" you called me to be. We know that by Faith, Abram received the promise. He became a change agent out of his passion and love for God. He drew his knife to slay his son, but God had a ram in the bush, for his faithfulness, for his work, his sacrifice, unto God. Then (Abram), now (Abraham) received great nations and Lived in the Promise. **"Lord, Don't Let Me Lose My Passion for you. I've got to Finish What I Started."**

Love, passion, and charity will cause you to have "Good Religion." Love, the Love of God, this Love, will make you do right even when you want to do wrong. The Passion of God, the Passion of Jesus Christ, will cause you to stand in there and "Fight for the Life that You Want." Love will cause you "To Get Back Up and Try it Again." If you have that true love, the Love of Jesus Christ, on the inside of you, the Passion of Christ, it will "Push you forward." It will drive you. It will cause you to not be weary in your well-doing, knowing that you will reap in due season if you faint not. Love will cause you to stand in there. It will cause your living not to be in vain. It will cause your giving not to be in vain. It will not let you waste your time. It will cause you to stay the Course, to go the distance. It will push you to "Finish What You Started." It's not over 'til God says it's over."

17

IT'S TIME TO CUT IT: CUT THE CORD

LUKE 9:59-62; REVELATION 14:4

John Mark accompanied Paul on his first missionary journey and is also the author of the book "Mark," who documented the initial prediction of Christ of his coming death.

 esus taught His disciples about His death and His resurrection. In confirmation of three's, Jesus forewarns his disciples of his death (Mark 8:31, 9:31, 10:33- 34). Jesus gives an illustration of the total submission required of his followers by the contrast of the cross in *(Mark 8:34) And when he had called the people unto Him with his disciples also, he said unto them, "Whosoever will come after me, let Him deny Himself, and take up his cross, and follow me."*

We find on this journey of life, this life of salvation, this walk following Christ, there are many ups, downs, standstills, waiting on God, moving forward, twists and turns, and gravitational pulls (only for the making of you). These moves of gravity will cause you to consider your true motive in following Christ. Is it for your own selfishness, vanity, lust, wants, or desires, or are you truly *Seeking the kingdom of God and his righteousness; that all these things shall be added unto you (Matthew 6:3).*

One thing about gravity is that it causes a shift by force, sometimes for good and possibly for the bad. Some forces of gravitational pulls can be critical on this journey of salvation. One must always remember not to allow the forces of the gravitational shifts to place doubt regarding your salvation, thus pulling you from the center. In fact, it should draw you to the center with the understanding that Christ is the center of it all.

When serving the Lord, you cannot allow distractions to set you back or send you back to where God called, pulled, and delivered you from. Likewise, you must be careful not to allow the gravitational pulls of your past failure, guilt, fear, shame, remorse, loss, betrayal, abuse, rejection, resentment, and unforgiveness to ruin your future in God.

At some point in time, God requires us to stand up boldly in the authority of Jesus Christ and stop the "devil" cold in his tracks and declare No More Will I Be a Victim of your tactics and your antics, for I AM more than a conqueror through Jesus Christ who has lifted me up out of a horrible pit, out of the miry clay, (despair) set my feet upon a rock and established my goings. (Psalm 40:2).

In the book of Matthew, in the 5th chapter, 27th-30th verse, Jesus teaches about lust. Figuratively speaking, he says, *"And if thy right hand offends thee, cut it off, and cast it from thee for it is profitable for thee that one of thy members should perish, and not that thy whole body should be cast into hell."* "It's Time to Cut It. Cut the Cord."

A simple statement: I'm getting out of the bed with the "devil." I will no longer be halted between two opinions, but I will pick up my bed and follow the Lord. I understand now that God cannot use me in the mindset of sliding back. It is time that I gird up and adjust myself moving forward to be of use to the "Kingdom of God," for it is at hand. It's time I do more than just believe in Him or on Him. But it's time I follow Him. "It's Time to Cut It. Cut the Cord." Cut the Cord to all ties of the devil. If there is anything found in me that is not like God, "It's Time to Cut It, Cut the Cord." Choke Him out, for I will no longer *be entangled again with the yoke of bondage (Galatians 5:1)* when freedom is encamped all around me. "It's Time to Cut It. Cut the Cord." Closing the door to those dead situations, those isms, and schisms, it is time to reject and *walk out of darkness and into the newness of light, having fellowship with Jesus Christ (1st John 3-7).* It is time to "Cut It. Cut the Cord."

Being in one accord, not on the cord, but in one accord on the day of Pentecost (Acts 2:1), Jesus called and is calling us to a *"radical commitment"* to following Him. You must be a willing worker, willing to leave where you once were and what you owned, denying yourself and your earthly wants and desires, picking up your cross, and following Him. Only by God's grace do we have this time!

Time. Through the dispensation of Grace, God has given us all time, this interval period, this measure of space from one point to another to get it right before the imposing of His judgment. While He clearly states, *"My Grace Is Sufficient,"* Paul *declared that he would take pleasure in his infirmities, in reproaches, in necessities, in persecutions for Christ's sake, for in our weakness, God is made Strong (2nd Corinthians 12:9).* In that time, I desire to be more than just a believer. I want to be more than just a hearer. My God is calling for a doer, doers of His Word. "It is time to Cut It. Cut the Cord."

Cutting the cord requires severing all forms of linkage, relationships, and blood flow, to all past associations, hang-ups, behaviors, attachments, and lifestyles. *For if any man be in Christ he is a new creature. Old things are passed away, behold all things are become new (2nd Corinthians 5:17).*

"It is Time to Cut It: Cut the Cord." It is time to get over yourself." It is time to stop allowing pride, sin, transgressions, iniquities, feelings, thoughts, emotions, and flesh to separate you from the love of Christ. It is time to "Cut It Out." Cut out playing with God, cut out pity-patting with the enemy. Jesus said you're either with Him or against Him (Luke 11:23). You're either on God's side or the enemy. You can't serve two masters; love one and hate the other, according to the scripture in Matthew 6:24.

In times like these, we all need our Savior. If my people, the people of God who have been called by my name, would humble themselves, and pray, seek my face, turn from their wicked ways, then shall I hear from heaven, forgive their sin, and will heal their lands (2nd Chronicles 7:14). Nine months after pregnancy there is child labor. After you have carried that baby, nurtured that baby, fed that baby, walked around with that baby attached to you, you give birth, and immediately following birth, it is "Time to Cut It: Cut the Cord." That is, detach it, if you will. Let it go for some; leave the cord behind for others. Move on, if you like. Leaving those former things behind me: I am pressing towards the mark for the prize of the high calling of God in Christ Jesus (Philippians 3: 13-14).

It is time to cut out anything that is not like Jesus, they say, that Lamb slain before the foundation of the world. Follow the Lamb wherever He may go (Revelation 14:4). Holy is the Lamb, the Lamb of God. It is time to give up your ways for his ways. The slogan says, "What Would Jesus Do?" Jesus gave up the Ghost on Calvary, a place called the "Skull," up on that rugged Cross at one point. To redeem man and make way for GRACE, he had to separate from the Father and "CUT IT." He had to "Cut the Cord"; the flesh had to die to allow the spirit to Rise Again. Yet I rise with all power. So, answer this question: Why is it so hard for us to cut the cord?

18

STAY WHERE YOU ARE AND GROW
HEBREWS 12:1-13

Many times, throughout the human life span, growth takes place, from conception to an embryo, while in utero, after birth. If there is life, growth continues to take place.

---

*I*n systematic stages, the phases of life must take place in order. The societal norm or statistical observation is that each phase must come simultaneously before or after another if you will. This equals normalities. We understand that when growth takes place out of order, irregularities show themselves in the scheme of things. It is classified as abnormal with the profound statement that it is **"Not Supposed to Be This Way."** Do we really understand that the higher the exaltation in God, the greater the sacrifices unto God you must give?

Most times, in the phases of abnormalities, individuals use this time to run away from the process of growth, choosing to run from their problems, situations, circumstances, and God's chastisement, whether rebuke, reproof, or correction, often failing to realize that sin has consequences. Falling out of the will of God requires correction in an effort to bring us back into God's will.

Why is it that when it's time to grow in God, when it's time to be corrected, trained, sometimes punished in love, to promote growth, we want to tell God how to teach us the lesson? Or do we run from the rod of correction? We want to question God about his methods, as Habakkuk, the prophet of Judah, cried out, "O Lord, how long shall I cry, and thou wilt not hear? Even cry out unto thee of violence, and thou wilt not save!" Habakkuk had questions:

1. Why does it seem that his people of Judah were doing evil and seemingly getting away with it? He wondered why God didn't punish them. After God's response to the (Chaldeans), those evil Babylonians being raised up to judge them,
2. Habakkuk questioned how God could use such violent, godless pagans to chastise his people. But even in his questioning of God, Habakkuk stood his ground in God. He said, "I will stand upon my watch, and set me upon the tower, and will watch to see what he will say unto me, and what I shall answer when I am "reproved" (rebuked), and the Lord answered Him and said, 'Write the vision and make it plain upon my tables, that he may run that readeth it.'"

Growth is a measurable yet immeasurable human characteristic that perpetuates endlessly at times. It can go on and on without a definite or defined end. According to Dictionary.com, the word grow is a verb and means of a living thing; undergo natural development by increasing in size and changing physically; progress to maturity. The further definition includes that the word grow means to become larger or greater over a period of time, to **increase**, so to speak.

When we think of *increase,* we know out of the descendants of Judah comes Jabez. Although his name signified that his mother bore Him in sorrow, we find out that Jabez was remembered for a heroic act of prayer unto God. In the midst of a dying and sinful world, we need to take the opportunity to ask the God of Israel, as Jabez did, to 1) Bless Me Indeed; 2) Enlarge my (coast) territory; 3) Thy Hand Be with Me and 4) Keep me from all evil that it may not grieve (harm) me. Are you praying for increase today? Are you inquiring of God with great expectancy that He will work it all out? We learned that Jabez got just what he requested of God: "Increase, O Lord. Bless Me Indeed."

The word increase, like growth, means to become greater. No doubt we ask for increase in God. We understand that God has no end. He is an infinite God. To infinity and beyond. He is eternal. He is everlasting to everlasting. Therefore, we must understand that when we try to measure the word grow, we look for (GROWTH) in every aspect, the act or manner or process of growing the size or stage of development that may include the completed stage of development. Do you enter with a presence of liberty (Freedom)? Where the Spirit of the Lord is, there is liberty (Freedom). Do you enter with a spirit of thanksgiving and of praise?

He is looking for those that bear the fruit of the tree, the fruits of the Spirit. Are you exemplifying growth in God? Are you being **Loving** today? Do you love your neighbor as yourself? Do you have **Joy,** unspeakable joy? Is the joy of the Lord your strength? He is seeking those that are following **peace** with all men, those that are living holy to see the Lord. Where are those showing patience, kindness, goodness, and faithfulness and those with self-control? There is no law against these areas of growth (Galatians 5:22-23).

I think this marks a matchless moment in the name of the Lord to say, "Stay Where You Are and Grow."

Time to Grow. We understand that the vision was only to come forth at an appointed time. God said it shall speak and not lie. Though it tarry, wait for it because it will surely come. It will not tarry, (Habakkuk 2:2). We understand that everything happens in seasons. "To everything there is a season and a time for every purpose under the heavens." Through observation, Solomon notes this in the book of Ecclesiastes 3:1. Solomon further makes valuable points that God has a plan. "Many are the devices within a man's heart, but only the counsel of the Lord shall prevail" (Proverbs 19:21).

In that plan, there is an appointed "TIME" for everything which comes forth in its season. The cycles of life help us to understand/or put into perspective why we know that all things work together for the good of them that love God and are called "according to His purpose" (Romans 8:28). At some point, you grow to the perspective of Habakkuk, "Yet I will rejoice in the Lord. I will joy in the God of my salvation. The Lord God is my strength, and He will make my feet like hinds' feet, and He will make me to walk upon mine high places. To the chief singer on my stringed instruments."

Paul expresses or alludes to a plan that God will work His plan out for you. If we go further, we find out that God has a plan. But it is only for those that love and believe in Him, those that can endure chastisement, those that are called and have accepted the call, those that are holy because He is holy; those that are living the right life, that have the right spirit; those righteous ones that He said He would withhold no good thing from the upright. Those that don't allow heartache, pain, and suffering to separate them from Him; those that yet press towards the mark; those that still have a "Yes" in their spirit. Those that are lifting holy hands and marvel at His good works; those that truly understand He will perfect that which is within you concerning Him all for his GLORY.

Always attentive unto our needs, Paul declared in Philippians 4:19,

> "But my God shall supply all your need," (no s, not plural, just "need"), according to His riches in glory by Christ Jesus. Wounded for our transgressions, bruised for my iniquities, the chastisement of my peace was upon Him and by His Stripes we are healed." God already made a way. The Song says God will make a way somehow. I Know the Lord will make a way. So, I'll just stay with Him and grow.

_____
_____
_____
_____
_____
_____
_____
_____
_____
_____
_____
_____
_____
_____
_____
_____
_____
_____

19

I GOT SOME MORE GROUND TO COVER

I AM GOING FOR THE FULLNESS OF GOD

1st Corinthians 10:26, Habakkuk 2:14, Isaiah 40:28-31

Seems not too long ago, on the first Sunday of 2016, the term was coined "Focused Dreamer with No Excuses." The true essence of this is that the desire to improve your life year after year begins in the heart of God. David said in Psalm 65:11, "Thou crowns (Surround me O Lord) the year with Thy goodness; and Thy paths drop fatness." In other words, drip with abundance. In the Bible days, "fatness" was considered a sign of material success. While in Kadesh, Moses sent twelve spies to the Promised Land to scout out whether it was "fat" or "lean" (Numbers 13:26-27). The spies brought back word that the land was flowing with milk and honey. What will it take for you to acquire the blessings of God in your life? I Got Some More Ground to Cover. I Am Going for the Fullness of God.

One should have gained insight on how to focus and overcome distractions. Not allowing negatives to cause you to lose sight of the positive. One should have learned to continue to dream, having faith and hope set above what you cannot see. One should be sick and tired and no longer have the desire to make excuses, but focusing and producing results should be the resolve.

There is a dichotomy in this coined term between thought and action, meaning a contrast between the two. A thought is simply just that, a thought. But there is something different when you take your thought and put it into action. Take your thought and put your focus on overcoming your distractions. To accomplish your dreams brings resolution to the outlined problem. There is nothing impossible in God, for, in God, all things are possible. "Focused Dreamers with No Excuses." Are you yet dreaming? Are you yet focused? Are you past making excuses?

> *Hast thou not known? Hast thou not heard that the everlasting God, the Lord, the Creator of the ends of the earth fainteth not, neither is weary? There is no searching of his understanding. He giveth power to the faint; and to them that have no might he increaseth strength. Even the youths shall grow weary, and the young men shall utterly fall. But they that wait upon the Lord shall renew their strength. They shall mount up with wings as eagles, they shall run and not be weary. They shall walk and not faint.*

With all that, one should have learned to be resilient in adversity, in trials and tribulations. Somebody should have learned how to STAND. One should have learned **upon Who** they STAND and in Whom they STAND, and **who/what** they STAND for.

For I am standing on the promise of God. I am standing

upon the Rock of my Salvation. I am standing in the Power of the Holy Ghost. I am standing in the Name of the Lord. I am standing for Jesus. After doing all that, you can STAND. If you're reading this, you are still standing. You are still here, and what the devil meant for your bad, for evil against you, God turned it for your good.

Understanding that, I have a little bit of wisdom now. The Word says, "Wisdom is the principle thing; therefore, get wisdom and in **All** thy getting, get understanding *(Proverbs 4:7)*. In other words, be clear, have clarity about what the Lord is saying unto the Church and what paths you ought to take. Are you waiting and listening to Him in this season? If you are still here, if you are still standing and not just existing, but having the right spirit and standing in the name of the Lord, then attest to this thought that I Got Some More Ground to Cover; I Am Going for the Fullness of God. I'm going for the abundance of his drops. I am in pursuit of his Glory- the manifestations of God's presence and the totality of his honor. "Let your light shine before men, that they may see your good works, and glorify your Father who is in heaven" (Matthew 5:16). For in Christ dwells the fullness of the Godhead bodily, for God dwells where there is Glory (Colossians 2:9). God dwells where his Glory is solicited. Where there is Glory, there is God. Breakthroughs, signs, and wonders shall follow them that believe. I got some more ground to cover. I am going for the fullness of God. The request of Jabez Enlarge my territory O Lord, do not let evil come upon me, and Lord Bless Me Indeed.

Ezekiel 34:26 *says, "And, I will make them and the places round about my hill a blessing, and I will cause the shower to come down in his season; there shall be showers of blessings."* We understand we must stay 'round about God to experience His glory. We have to make sure that it is truly all about Him. We have to be careful in which paths we're going to take because only God's paths drip with fatness. It is only the counsel of the Lord that shall prevail. In everything, He must get the glory.

Jesus gave us, the Body of Christ, all the baptized believers, members of His body, a directive in (Matthews 28:19) *to go yea therefore teaching all nations, baptizing them in the name of the Father, of the son and of the Holy Ghost.* I believe we have to spread the gospel, the good news of Jesus Christ, telling somebody He still saves, heals, and delivers. Tell them that Jesus yet lives on the inside of me. I Got Some More Ground to Cover. I Am Going for the Fullness of God. I count not myself to have apprehended, nor do I want to be a castaway. I'm yet in the race, and I have more ground to cover. The earth is the Lord's and the fullness thereof.

I have some more ground to cover, some hedges and highways to attract, some gaps that I must bridge, some seeds that I must plant, some ground I must till.

Romans 8:18-25

Wait to remain inactive or in a state of repose until something expected happens.

Expectancy- the quality or state of expecting; expectation; anticipatory belief or desire.

Promise-an expressed assurance on which expectation is to be based.

Daniel Fast- waiting on a move of God.

_____
_____
_____
_____
_____
_____
_____

20

WAIT ON HIM WITH GREAT
EXPECTANCY

But if we hope for that what we see not, then we do with
patience wait for it. I believe that by now many of us have all
come to the realization that endurance is a required trait or
philosophy a school of thought that we all must have in this
walk of life and on this Christian journey of salvation.

— *ROMANS 8:25*

he scripture reflects in *Hebrews 10:36, For ye have*
need of patience, (endurance) that, after ye have done
the will of God, ye might receive the promise. The old cliché
that "Patience is a Virtue" rings out clearly in my mind.
Understanding that patience is not only a virtue, but it is a
requirement in serving God because in order to receive the
promises of God, part of the process is to WAIT on Him. The
song says that serving the Lord will pay off after a while. The
Bible says, *(Therefore being justified by faith, we have peace with*
God through our Lord Jesus Christ: By whom also we have access

by faith into this grace wherein we stand and rejoice in hope of the glory of God. And not only so, but we glory in tribulations also: knowing that tribulations worketh patience; And patience, experience: and experience, hope: Romans 5:1-4). Paul gives us an idealization that there is a way to wait on God, and murmuring and complaining, moaning and groaning, is not it. **SHOUT: Your problems, Your trials, and Your tribulations are to help you GROW. Take a little Room to Grow; God is still working on me.** He still perfecting that thing within me concerning Him. I just need a little Room to GROW....

"Patience is a way of life," David said, I waited patiently upon the Lord and he heard my cry and he inclined unto me (Psalm 40). Just because God didn't move when or how you wanted Him to move doesn't mean he did not hear you, but God moves in his own time, for he is God.

In everything in life, there is a process; most would say that processes take time. **To everything there is a season and time to every purpose.**

Many times, we must trust the process. Often, we fail to trust God while in the process, and we become weary in our well-doing, causing us to lose focus, and patience runs out for some. Waiting on Him with great expectancy requires one to have patience, that endurance that goes all the way to the end. Understanding that if he did it before, he will do it again. Isn't it something how we have trusted God before, and for some reason, we question Him now? He is the same God back then that he is right now. For He said in his word that **I am the Lord and I change not, (Malachi 3:6).**

Waiting with great expectancy is a testament of faith, applied belief; that is, faith in action. This allows you to reminisce or remember the time He brought you out repeatedly, so now you should marvel at His wonderful and mighty works and wait in faith on what He will do in your future. *Beloved, I wish above all things that thou mayest prosper and be in health, even as thy soul prospereth (3 John:2).*

We can't even comprehend. Paul writes what God has in store for those that endure until the end. We can't even begin to fathom the thought of this life or eternity. So, we wait in hope.

Are you waiting in great expectancy on Him? God is doing great things. God is great and greatly to be praised. He is sovereign in all His ways. He is in control. He is above all things. Like Him, there is no other. I am waiting in great expectancy. *"For all the promises of God in Him are yea, and in Him Amen, unto the glory of God by us."* Job 14:14 had a question: *"Shall a man die? Shall he live again?" He said, "All the days of my appointed time wilt I wait until my change come" (2nd Corinthians 1:20).* Are you waiting on God? Are you waiting until your change comes? Are you waiting until God changes your situation? Are you waiting in expectancy on God to change your circumstances? I am waiting in expectancy.

_____

_____

_____

_____

_____

_____

_____

_____

_____

_____

_____

_____

_____

_____

_____

_____

21

I AM LOADED

I am on a mission, an assignment of evangelism by God, built upon the principalities of the Bible, to spread the Good News, the gospel, the doctrine of Jesus Christ, His death, burial and resurrection.

This is for the believers today. Well, we understand that to see Him, by faith, we must first believe that He is and that He is a rewarder of them that diligently seek Him **(Hebrews 11:6).** Are there any believers today? Do you know who God is and that our Redeemer yet lives? Are you in a relationship with God? The best way to tell somebody about God and who God is is to tell of the goodness of Jesus. Has he done anything for you lately?

Baffled, confused, and mystified by the God-given topic, I just went with the mission of God to say, "*I AM LOADED. I AM LOADED.*" We understand the word Loaded has a variety of meanings that include bearing or having a load; full or containing ammunition or an explosive charge. Scratching my head for the last couple of weeks, God said, *"I AM LOADED." Blessed be the name of the Lord who loads us with benefits" (Psalm 68:19).*

I AM LOADED. When reading the text, we find Nicodemus asked a question: "How can a man be born when he is old? Can he enter the second time into his mother's womb and be born?" Jesus answered, "Verily, verily, I say unto thee, except a man be born of water and of the Spirit, he cannot enter into the kingdom of God. That which is born of the flesh is flesh and that which is born of the Spirit is spirit."

Questions to Answer: Have you been born again? Are you loaded today? I found out that **I AM** introduced Himself to Moses at the burning bush as the God of thy Father, the God of Abraham, the God of Isaac, and the God of Jacob **(Exodus 3:6)**. The I AM said I AM that I AM, and I AM loaded. I Am the bread of life, for in the beginning was the Word and the Word was with God, and the Word was God (John 1:1). I AM Loaded. If the I Am dwells on the inside of you, then you can profess that I AM Loaded. I Am Loaded with power, love, joy, and peace, for the I AM resides within Me.

_____

_____

_____

_____

_____

_____

_____

_____

_____

_____

_____

_____

22

I'VE GOT SOMETHING TO PROVE

Proving something, proof of something. **Proof** *demonstrates the truth or existence of something by evidence or argument; an act of accountability and application.*

e see here, by way of scripture, that God is seeking proof *"as a refiner and purifier of silver."* He will *"purify the sons of Levi, purge them as gold and silver that they may offer up to the Lord an offering of righteousness."* This raw metal must go through the process of purification, being heated with fire, melting, separating, and skimming of impurities, leaving pure metal to be proven. *"I Got Something to Prove."* God further directs his people by instruction in the *10th verse of Malachi, third chapter, "To prove me now herewith, saith the Lord of Hosts."* God only requires of us what he has already given, which is your life in its totality. Giving is a natural response of **LOVE!**

He gave his son that we might believe and give Him our life. *"For God so loved the world that he gave his only begotten Son that whosoever believed on Him should not parish but have everlasting life. (John 3:16).* He said, "Give and it shall be given unto you" (Luke 6:38). Love is a word of action. It is a testament that requires **PROOF.** You said you "Love God." Prove it.

The proof led me to this commonly used statement dating back to the 1920s. It increased in popularity of use in the United States in the 1950s, "The Proof is in the Pudding." This short proverb phrase is clear and concise in meaning by way of an analogy that we may understand that you can only determine if something is a success or not after it has been tried, tested out, and used in all it has to be proven. *(The song says, I have gone through the fire, and I've been through the flood, I've been broken into pieces, seen lightning flashing from above. But through it all, I remember that He loves me, and He cares, and He'll never put more on me than I can bear).* The only way to be Proven is that you must be Used, Tested and Tried, Beat Up, Busted and Disgusted, Lied On, Cheated, Talked About, Mistreated, Up, Down, Almost Level to the Ground, but will you Stand to be Proven?

Therefore, Beloved, think it not strange concerning the fiery trials which are to try you, as though some strange thing happened unto you: But rejoice, in as much as ye are partakers of Christ's sufferings; that when his glory shall be revealed, ye may be glad also with exceeding joy! **(1 Peter 4:12-13)**

In life, the majority rule would agree that everything must be proven, tested, and tried to determine its validity. It doesn't matter if it is people, places, or things. Everything has a process to determine its authenticity.

A hypothesis is a statement in the form of a question that needs answering that requires further investigation. The hypothesis requires predictions to determine if a theory is correct or not. It is a tentative and tested statement about how changes in one thing are expected to explain the changes in something else. For example, the theory is the "More I Praise

Him, the Better I Feel." *The hypothesis predicts the variables in a statement, and here are the two variables of this statement: (1), The More I Praise Him; (2), The Better I Feel.*

We understand that these variables vary together, meaning that they both have something in common: They have a relationship. They have association and change in one. It brings about a change in the other. One is a **cause,** and the other is the **effect.** One is independent, and the other is dependent.

Understand that the independent variable causes the change, and the dependent variable is the effect of the change. Going back to our example, "The More I Praise Him, the Better I Feel," the More I Praise Him" is the independent variable. The effect is "The Better I Feel." Everything has a process of being proven.

He said in Luke 12:48, "For unto whomsoever much is given, much is required" (Independent). So, because He gave/gives you (Dependent), you have a requirement. Yes, I Got Something to Prove. I Got Something to Prove. The more responsibility, the greater the expectancy of you, and the more resources, talent, and understanding God gives you, the more responsible and efficient we should prove ourselves to be unto Him. Paul said, "Be not conformed to this world: but be ye transformed by the renewing of your mind, that ye may prove what is that good and acceptable and perfect will of God" (Romans 12:2). When we understand the cause and effect of change, you understand the process that not being conformed to this world and being transformed can only take place once your Mind is Renewed. Once your mind is renewed, now "I Got Something to Prove." Now I can "Study to show thyself approved unto God a workman that not needeth to be ashamed, rightly dividing the word of truth" (2 Timothy 2:15). "From this cause I abide in Him that his words can abide in me. I can ask what I will, and it shall be given unto me" (John 15:7).

This life is unscripted. The road map to Heaven lies in the

Living Word of God (66 books, 39 in the old and 27 in the new), and the only way is to keep his commandments, for obedience is better than sacrifice. The hour is drawing nigh for you to decide and prove if you're living for God or not, with the understanding that we must live out what we decided because God will examine what kind of workers we have all been for and unto Him.

As God continues to prove Himself to you, you have a requirement, a responsibility to prove yourself unto Him, *let every man examine yourselves, whether ye be in faith; prove your own selves. Know ye not your own selves, how that Jesus Christ is in you, except ye be reprobates? (2nd Corinthians 13:5), (Galatians 6:4) But let every man prove his own work, and then shall he have rejoicing in Himself alone, and not in another. Examine. Prove your own actions. Are you a true Christian or are you an imposter? For Judgement will begin at the house of God: and if it first began at us, what shall the end be of them that obey not the gospel of God? 18 And if the righteous scarcely be saved, where shall the ungodly and the sinner appear? (1 Peter 4:17-18)*

As God continues to prove Himself to you, you have a requirement and a responsibility to prove yourself unto Him (Job 23:10 says, "But He knoweth the way that I take: when He hath tried me, I shall come forth as gold."

> Have you been tried in the fire? Yes.
> Have you been tried in the fire? Yes.
> Have you been tried in the fire? Yes.
> Did you come through as pure gold?
> I've got something to prove! Psalm 34:1-2

_____

_____

_____

_____

23

GET OVER YOURSELF AND LIFT UP
THE NAME OF JESUS

God woke me up with this one here out of my sleep from an unexpected nap on a Friday late afternoon with my grandbaby in my arms. He woke me up in the spirit, saying, "Get Over Yourself."

---

*F*alling back to sleep, He woke me until I logged in my notes "Get Over Yourself." Playing around with it in my head, I could hear God repeatedly saying, "Get Over Yourself," and then came, "Lift Up the Name of Jesus." Then I kept hearing the song "Victory Belongs to Jesus. Victory belongs to Him." If you will just say if you mean Heaven all the way, and you have a made-up mind, and you know you were created for the glory of the Lord, "Get Over Yourself and Lift Up the Name of Jesus." You wanted a word today, well, there it is, for it is the day of the Lord. I will rejoice in it.

When defining, Get Over Yourself means stop wallowing in self-pity and start doing something about what is eating you. This statement can act as a word of caution to someone who is too absorbed in his/her own self and fails to look beyond that limited perspective. It relates to an inflated sense of self-importance, whether positive or negative. The question today is, when did it ever become all about you? The answer is it never was. It is truly all about God who gave his only begotten Son that we might all be redeemed.

It is too often, and the hour is drawing nigh to indulge in putting Jesus on the back burner for the cares of this world. We say that we love Him, worship, and adore Him; however, living contradictory to His word. He said, **"Take no thought for your life, what ye shall eat, or what ye shall drink; nor what ye shall put on. Is not the life more than meat, and raiment?" (Matthew 6:25).** Isn't it funny how we confuse these two? **Worry and Genuine Concern.** There is a difference when you become immobilized by your problems, issues, adversities, and circumstances and when your needs and wants take precedence over lifting the name of the Lord. Consumed with thoughts of self and Worry, you find that individuals fall out of God, miss out on prayer time, fasting time, and church time dealing with issues that we say we "turned over to the Lord to work out." Pastor Willie J. Wimbush, Jr. and I preached a message If You're Going to Worry, then Why Pray? When you have genuine concerns and have truly turned your life over to the Lord to work it out, you are moved to action and will lift up the name of Jesus through the process.

Do we know that God is attentive to those that call on Him, to those that believe, love, and trust in Him? Do you know that God is not slack concerning his promises? Whether He makes a way of escape from trouble or helps us in the time of trouble, He hears and answers prayer. He is a rewarder to those that diligently seek Him.

A testament to no matter what you go through or deal with, we find in our text this familiar and often quoted scripture that David said, *"I will Bless the Lord at all times and his praise shall continually be in my mouth. My soul makes her boast in the Lord. The humble shall hear thereof and be glad."* David did not put a limitation, a stipulation, or a condition on when he would Bless the Lord, for he said he would Bless the Lord at all times because he understood it was not about himself.

We find that David took thought and had great concern about his life. He had to stay alive. He had to keep on living, as we all must keep on living because, as David was, we all are living with a death threat. His was by Saul; ours is of the devil, your adversary who seeks to (kill, steal and destroy). We find that David ran for his life, hiding in caves, living with the enemy, those Philistines, to the point of playing crazy in front of King Achish *(1 Samuel 21:10-15)*. Nevertheless, he was moved by purpose and driven by divine destiny to survive because it was never about Him but about someone greater than "I," someone that was coming through the bloodline of his lineage by the name of Jesus, the coming Messiah, the Savior of the world, the way, truth, and life.

Colossians 2:12-14, Colossians 1:12-14 (Paul, to combat errors and heresies in the Church, let believers know that in Christ, we have all that we need).

24

WHAT DIFFERENCE DID THE CROSS
MAKE AFTER THE CRUCIFIXION?
LIVING THE AFTERMATH!

What difference did the cross make? The cross, this upright
post used as an instrument of death in ancient times? The
cross is used as means of the atonement made between God
and humanity.

he old rugged, approximately 300-pound cross, that
horizontal bar known as the patibulum (crossbar),
had a weight of between 75 and 125 pounds. We must add in the
weight of our transgressions. This cross is where our Savior
hung, bled, gave up the ghost, and died a horrible death by
crucifixion. The cross of **Crucifixion,** this historical method of
capital punishment initiated by the Phoenicians and later
adopted by the Roman Empire, in which the victim is tied or
nailed to a large wooden beam and left to hang for several days
until eventual death from exhaustion and asphyxiation.
Asphyxiation means the state or process of being deprived of
oxygen, which can result in unconsciousness or death by
suffocation. What difference did the cross make?

In the old testament book of *Psalm 22,* David, early on, described unknowingly the death of Jesus the Christ by way of crucifixion before crucifixion even became a way of punishment. *"For the dogs have compassed me: the assembly of the wicked have enclosed me. They pierced my hands and my feet. I may tell all my bones: they look and stare upon me. They part my garments among them and cast lots upon my vesture."* Rejected, beaten, tortured, reviled, humiliated, and naked, he would endure the cross through suffering, pain, and agony. What difference did the cross make? The cross made all the difference, for the cross represents love for all humanity because, according to John, ***"God so loved the world that he gave his only begotten son that whosoever believed on Him shall not perish but have everlasting life" (John 3:16).*** The cross represents the redemption of man through the blood of Jesus Christ. The cross was not by happenstance, but the cross was the divine action plan of God being Christ manifested in the flesh to redeem man from his own self-inflicted sins by way of reconciliation. *"Therefore, if any be in Christ, he is a new creature. Old things are passed away and behold all things become new. And all things are of God, who hath reconciled us to Himself by Jesus Christ, and hath given to us the ministry of reconciliation; To wit, that God was in Christ, reconciling the world unto Himself, not imputing their trespasses unto them; and have committed unto us the word of reconciliation" (2 Corinthians. 5:17-19).* The cross made all the difference. No cross, no crown.

After the carrying the cross and the weight of sin nailed to it, after the crucifixion, after being lead as a lamb to the slaughter, after being wounded for my transgressions, bruised for my iniquities, after the chastisement of my peace be upon Him, after being oppressed and afflicted, after not saying a mumbling word, after the Crucifixion, *"Wherefore seeing we are compassed about with so great a cloud of witnesses, let us lay aside every weight that so easily beset us, and run with patience this race that is set before us, looking unto Jesus who is the Author and the Finisher of our faith; who for the joy that was set before Him endured the cross, despising the shame, and is sat down at the right hand of God" (Hebrews 12:1-2), after he paid it all, after the Cross and after the Crucifixion,* after the death, burial and resurrection, after death has no sting and the grave no victory comes the aftermath. I Am living the aftermath. The aftermath takes place as the after-effects of a significant unpleasant event. After the Christ died upon the cross, after the crucifixion, the pardon of my transgressions, Paul lists the aftermath (Col 1:12-14) of the cross, the crucifixion, the benefits after (1) he made us fit, (meet) the cross made us qualified to be partakers of the Kingdom of God. He said in 2nd Corinthians 5:20-21 that we are ambassadors of Jesus Christ. I am a messenger of Jesus Christ. I now have a mission of the apostles' doctrine to tell somebody about our Redeemer, our Reconciler, that He yet lives, yet saves. He made a pardon for my sins and made me the righteousness of God. I am living the aftermath. (2) He rescued us, delivered us from the power of darkness, and made us His children in the body of His flesh through death, to present you holy and unblameable and unreproveable in His sight. (3) He gave us a place in the eternal kingdom of God. (4) He redeemed us; he purchased our freedom. He was the ransom to set us free. It was by His own blood that He obtained redemption. (5) He forgave all our sins and cleansed us from all unrighteousness. I Am living the aftermath. My old man is crucified with Him, and the body of sin is destroyed. I am no longer a servant of sin (Romans 6:6), for the wages of sin is death, but the gift of God is eternal life through Jesus Christ our Lord, the firstborn from the dead, the head of the Body, the Church. I AM living the aftermath. Oh, how it pleased the Father, for in Him should all fullness dwell and having made peace through the blood of His cross, by Him to reconcile all things unto Himself; (Colossians 1:19-20).

I Am living the aftermath. Psalm 133:1, Ephesians 4:1-6.

_____

_____

_____

_____

_____

_____

_____

_____

_____

_____

_____

_____

_____

_____

_____

_____

_____

_____

_____

_____

_____

_____

_____

_____

_____

_____

_____

_____

_____

_____

_____

_____

25

WOMEN IN UNITY

WHAT IS THE POSTURE OF YOUR HEART?

There is a clear understanding that the unity within the Body of Christ is strained, shaken, and not abounding as it should while the foundation lays solid and assures the people of God are caught up in themselves and struggling to hold to a fixed belief. To add, people have disagreements, sow discord, discredit one another and cause division among the ranks over unimportant issues.

omen in Unity, what is Your Heart's Posture? There is something to understand that when you start to describe unity amongst the brethren(Women), we must first determine the posture of one's own heart. Why? Because there is a direct correlation between unity and the posture of one's heart. There is a mutual connection between unity and the heart's posture. For unity, U-N-I-T-Y is defined as the state and/or the ability to join together; the state of being one; oneness, if you will. It is the totality of being a whole. But without having a posture, unity cannot be obtained. The word posture, as a noun, is a particular way of dealing with or considering something, an approach, or attitude. Posture as a verb is to behave in a way intended to impress or mislead others. So if we pause right there and ask you a question, it would be, what is your heart's posture? What is your stance on God? What is your approach or attitude towards unification, i.e., unity?

The realization is that for one to have unity, you must first have the right posture, the right spirit. Your posture must be pure for there is something about AUTHENTICITY that resonates abroad. There is something about the **"pure in heart."** The Bible says, *"They shall see God," Matthew 5:8.* It is something about "Keeping it Real." What is the posture of your heart?

Women, this female gender, this human being created by Elohim, the God of Israel, this mother of the earth taken out of man, bone of Adam's bone, and flesh of his flesh, struggle with the validity of who she is. So often, she falls into needing the validation of others, allowing what others think or say to dictate her reality. Struggling to die to her own insecurities, living in false pretenses of her own reality, can we just "Keep It Real?" Because there is no "Future in your Frontin" (McBreed). The only way to walk in unity is to be true to who and whose you are. **Amos 3:3** asked, "**Can two walk together except they be agreed?**" To have unity, you must have agreement; you must be cohesive one with another in one accord.

Women in Unity, what is your heart's posture? What is your motive, your modus operandi behind what you do? Are you doing what you do to be seen for your own fame or fortune or because you have been captivated and enslaved by the gospel of Jesus Christ that you do what you do to the GLORY of God? What is the posture of your heart? Isn't it something that *"Eli looked upon the outward appearance of Hannah and assumed that she was drunken and not that woman of a sorrowful heart, that cried out before the Lord"? 1 Samuel 1:12-15. But God! "The Lord looked upon the heart," 1 Samuel 16:7.* I believe unity and her heart's posture got her heart's desire, and Samuel came forth.

David said in our scripture text, *Psalm 133:1, "Behold (see/observe), (watch this), how good and how pleasant it is for brethren to dwell together in unity!"* David's description of a harmonious (free from disagreement and dissent), pleasant relationship is the outward expression of unity that reflects our inward unity of purpose. There is something about a tuneful lack of discord relationship that pleases the Lord. This relationship built upon joy, love, peace, meekness, kindness, gentleness, long-suffering, and patience forms a wholeness, a cohesive bond in the Lord. It allows room for purpose to arise and reflect on the world. Unity allowed Ruth, the Moabitess woman, wife of Mahlon, to acculturate to the land, the people, and the God of Naomi (hope within), the posture of Ruth's heart (steadfastly made up/loyalty). Check it. What is your heart's posture?

_____
_____
_____
_____
_____
_____
_____
_____
_____
_____
_____
_____
_____
_____
_____
_____
_____

26

WOMEN WALKING IN DESTINY
I WILL TAKE NOTHING FOR MY JOURNEY

Participation Is Required Here. Right now, at this very moment in your lifespan, 1. ask yourself or link up with someone and say, "How did (I/you) get here?"

This is a question in life we have all asked ourselves at one time or another. You look around at your own circumstances or calamities and say, **"How did I get here?"**

In a review from the Book of Joel, the son of Pethuel, Prophet of the Judah Nation, the Southern Kingdom, writes to press upon, to warn Judah of the judgment of God because of their sins, to urge them to repent and turn back to God. Deeming the things you have dealt with to be **"Necessary"** to redirect you back to God. It is something when we forget that God appealed in those days as He is in these days in *Joel 1:2. "Hear this, ye old men, and give ear, all ye inhabitants of the land, Hath this been in your days, or even in the days of your Fathers"? Joel 1:3 "Tell your children of it, and let your children tell their children, and their children another generation." Joel 1:4, "that* *which the palmerworm hath left, the locust eaten, and that which the locust hath left the cankerworm eaten; and that which the cankerworm hath left the caterpillar eaten." Finally, in Joel 1:5, "the Prophet gives a wakeup call to the people "awake, ye drunkards," and weep; and howl, all ye drinkers of wine, because of the new wine, for it is cut off from "your mouth."*

Joel's prediction is what happens when we fail to surrender to God, thus leading to judgment being imposed. **The Valley of Decision is a reality.** The Valley of God's Judgement is real; just look around you. It appears somebody failed to educate themselves and to tell somebody and somebody failed to listen to the message that He will have no other gods before Him. Well, glory be to God that school is still in session. It only behooves us to get the lesson while the Teacher is yet teaching. Women/Men, young and old, we have a responsibility to surrender our lives to the Lord by the declaration of God and to spread the **Good News of Jesus Christ.** We have been charged to **Choose this day who we will serve, and there can only be One Master.** We must thank God for His sovereignty, grace, and mercy that He has bestowed upon us. The kindness He extends out of Agape love allows us to journey back unto Him. The beautiful thing is that He teaches us how to come back to Him, as He does here in Joel 2:12, *Therefore also now, saith the Lord, our ye even to me with all your heart, and with fasting, and praying, and weeping, and with mourning: And rend your heart, and not your garments, and turn unto the Lord your God: for he is gracious and merciful, slow to anger, and of great kindness, and repenteth Him of evil.*

Women, be willing to take your journey and negate being a victim anymore of your circumstances because the path of life is an Odyssey of spiritual events that reminds us of who we are, connected to a journey, a long and often challenging process of personal change and development to foster growth.

Destiny - the hidden power believed to control what will happen in the future. In other words, it is fate. The Bible teaches that Man was created with the ability to make moral choices and that he is responsible for those choices. The Fall of man was not a predetermined event in which Adam and Eve were hapless victims of a Puppet-Master God. Quite the contrary. Adam and his wife (Women) had the ability to choose **Obedience** (with its attendant blessing) or **Disobedience** (with its consequent curse). They knew what the result of their decision would be, and they were held accountable (Genesis 3). 1st Corinthians 15:22, in Adam, all die. But in Christ, we are made alive.

Your participation requires you to spread the word loudly and with the compassion of a heart-felt voice of thought and tell everyone. We all had a **journey, but I chose my own destiny, and my journey was not always easy.**

Navigation Systems (Siri) sometimes make mistakes and lead you down the wrong paths. I have learned that in my own navigation, I did not and still don't have it altogether. I have been through many things in the game we call **LIFE**. So, you, like me, find it evident that you had a journey that led you to the House of the Lord; some paths and routes were harder than others. Some of the ravens of life were low, high, treacherous, dangerous, risky, uncomfortable, compromising, unlawful, ungodly, downright sinful, unfair, heart aching and heartbreaking, painful, deep, "Why me" at times. And don't forget about those things that you said, "I will take it to my grave because I am too ashamed to tell anybody." Listen, *take nothing for your journey because in the end, you chose destiny. You chose to live and not die.*

27

I AIN'T LETTING GO OF MINE

(RELATIONSHIP)

Genesis 3:8-11, Genesis 3:24, Genesis 32:24-31

---

*A*fter reading our lesson text, let us focus on the concept of the word known as Relationship.

Relationship is defined as a connection, association, or involvement; connection between persons by blood or marriage; an emotional or other connection between people, with an understanding that all of what we do throughout this lifespan, including our daily activities of going and coming as we please, come down to one important key value and that is a relationship. We find that since the beginning, in Genesis, God strongly desired a relationship with us. Even though he knew man had sinned, he yet called out to Adam, "Where art thou?" SIN made Adam afraid, and SIN caused Adam to hide. SIN convinced them that their way was better than God's. SIN compromised this relationship and lays at the doorstep to attempt to destroy ours.

Individuals have taken the time to sit down and plan what

one considers relationship goals, definitively known as **Couple Goals.** One's opinion means to be happy and content in your relationship with someone. The **goal** is to be with someone who genuinely knows you and loves you with no judgment whatsoever. The relationship that has love, patience, tolerance, and security. Individuals have taken the time to sit down and analyze and thoughtfully plan out their personal relationship goals. They have identified the likes and dislikes, the do's and don'ts, what I will and what I won't tolerate, the financial parameters, if they will accept children or not, if they will have children or not, where do we see ourselves in five years. Now, there is careful goal setting for some in their Natural Relationships. But the fact of the matter is these relationships are TEMPORAL. For life is a vapour that appears for a little time and then vanisheth away. The question that remains is, do you have a relationship with God? Let's go a step further. How is your relationship with Him? Are you setting goals? Is your relationship building? Is it reciprocal? Are you sowing into your relationship what you desire to get back? Are you making excuses and self-defenses? Are you hiding from God? Are you convinced that God's way is the best? How is your relationship with God?

I understand that in setting relationship goals, one factor entails revisiting the goals, especially in times of turbulence. The question then becomes, how do we make this thing work? How do we stay together? So many people hold on to toxic, unhealthy relationships for their mind, body, and soul. At the risk of losing their sanity, people yet hold onto relationships with people, places, and things that are not advantageous for them nor have a profitable or beneficial outcome. But why is this same principle or manner/mode of operation not applied in the Body of Christ to fight, to hold onto our relationship with God? Why is it that someone must encourage, prime, plead and beg individuals to hold on in your daily relationship with

Christ to whom we say we love? Why does someone have to remind you to think back on all that he has done for you to ignite within you to hold onto your relationship? Why do we not read the warning signs when it yells DANGER of a BAD BREAKUP lies ahead? Do we understand that this should be a burning desire that resonates from the inside of us so deep that you cry out as Jacob did that I will not let go until you Bless Me? No, I ain't GOING OUT LIKE THAT. "I ain't letting go of mine." My relationship is too valuable. I have a lot at stake, a lot to lose out on, if I forsake my relationship with my Father, which art in Heaven. I stand to miss out on the promise. My seat in Heaven is in jeopardy if I forego my relationship with Christ.

We find in our lesson text that Jacob was in a relationship with God. Isn't it something that he had PERSISTENCE in this spiritual relationship that enacted Him to stay in the condition of the struggle with God and to COMMUNICATE what he needed out of this relationship, and that was to be Blessed? Jacob's unwillingness to let go of his relationship during the struggle allowed his character to be built, gave Him power with God, and allowed his name to be changed from a deceiver by descent to Israel, meaning the prince who struggles with God and prevails. Many saints/believers today are in the struggle of their lives in their own personal relationship with God to remain loyal to Him and to wait on the coming of the Messiah. Somebody would agree and say the struggle is real, but God! "I ain't letting go of mine." This is **NO LONGER A CHRISTIAN EXPERIENCE but a RELATIONSHIP, a FIGHT of the FITTEST.**

28

DON'T BE A STRANGER TO YOURSELF

Stranger: _____
Who Am I: _____

> *12 Wherefore, my beloved, as ye have always obeyed,*
> *not as in my presence only, but now much more*
> *in my absence, work out your own salvation*
> *with fear and trembling.*
> *13 For it is God which works in you both to will and*
> *to do of his good pleasure.*
> *14 Do all things without murmurings and*
> *disputing's:*
> *15 That ye may be blameless and harmless, the sons*
> *of God, without rebuke, in the midst of a crooked*
> *and perverse nation, among whom ye shine as*
> *lights in the world;*
> *16 Holding forth the word of life; that I may rejoice in*
> *the day of Christ, that I have run not in vain,*
> *neither labored in vain.*

— PHILIPPIANS 2:12-15

"Work out your own salvation," the Church working together to remove themselves from both division and discord.

1. Obey Christ. In this text, referring to obeying Christ, Paul, as the author, speaks to the Church of Philippi that they must not only be obedient in his presence as a leader. He would no longer be present to nudge them, but out of his presence, and most importantly, obedience should initiate in the presence of God.

2. One would ask, when nobody is watching you with the physical eye, are you careful to obey God?

3. We find in the 13th verse that God has not left us to struggle on our own in carrying out his will. He is there leading and navigating us through. He wants to live within us in an effort to help us obey Him and follow through.

4. True obedience must start with being changed and having the spirit of Christ, in part, with a passion for seeing God's will fulfilled. So Paul wrote during his imprisonment Philippians 1:19, "For I know that this shall turn to my salvation through your prayer, and the supply of the Spirit of Jesus Christ." Then, facing possible release or execution, he trusted that God would work it out.

5. Faithful obedience to God is best understood when you Do it, and you're not **"Just Exposed to It."** Observe, Interpret, and Application are clear terminologies of steps to enact obedience. Paul wrote in Philippians 4:8-9, "Finally, brethren, whatsoever things are true, whatsoever things are honest, whatsoever things are just, whatsoever things are pure, whatsoever things are lovely,

whatsoever things are of good report if there be any
virtue, and if there be any praise, think on these
things. Those things, which ye have both learned,
and received, and heard, and seen in me do and the
"God of peace shall be with you."

Focus on God is "Key" when it comes to obedience. "What
you put in your mind, body, and spirit is what you get out!" So
this year, recognize God and his true calling for (YOU) and
don't be a Stranger to Yourself.

1. Acknowledge (YOUR) shortcomings and rid
   yourself of preconceived thoughts of failure. Be
   aware of (YOUR OWN) strengths and weaknesses;
   this includes your limitations. Yes! the "Hard
   Stuff," the "Hard Questions," and the "Hard
   Realities of Knowing Thyself." This requires you to
   be true to who you are. Understand that what
   others think of you is not what is important.
   Impressionable? Maybe. But learn your self-worth.
   Learn your net worth in God and what he says
   about YOU! For he said, (Jeremiah 29:11-12), "For I
   know the thoughts that I think toward you, saith
   the Lord, thoughts of peace, and not of evil, to give
   you an expected end. Then shall ye call upon me,
   and ye shall go and pray unto me, and I will
   hearken unto you. And ye shall seek me, and find
   me, when ye shall search for me with all your
   heart."

2. Part of not being a "Stranger to Yourself," you accept
   that one often busy bodies in another man's affairs!
   Proverbs 19:21 sums it up by allowing God to Do IT!
   There are many devices in a man's heart;
   nevertheless, the Lord's counsel shall stand. Only

what is going to bring God Glory will happen! Allow Him to perfect that which concerns Him.

3. Know that God is the source of your Strength. As Pastor Willie J. Wimbush Jr. quoted, taken from Star Wars, "I Am One with the Force and Force is One with Me." Know Your Source and the Force that lies within you. The HOLY GHOST is the "source of God's Force" within You. So, don't be a "Stranger to Yourself." Be True to who you are and walk in the "Favor of God," Do his Will that his Glory may be Fulfilled in You!

_____

_____

_____

_____

_____

_____

_____

_____

_____

_____

_____

_____

_____

_____

_____

_____

_____

_____

_____

_____

_____

_____

29

GIVING BACK

"*G*iving Back" *is a coined term that many individuals use and abide in as a way of life, while a great number of others struggle to buy into for many different rhymes of* reason.

Let's list why it is a struggle for some of you to "Give Back."

1. _____
2. _____
3. _____
4. _____
5. _____
6. _____

Giving is defined as to freely transfer the possession of (something) to (someone); hand over to.

Back, in this regard, is used as a verb denoting an action that must take place to give financial, material, or moral support. Giving back is not to be stingy, prideful, complaining, showing off, worldly gain, or begrudging, but acts of love, compassion, caring, sharing, humane, graceful, and freely giving.

What does "Giving Back" mean to you?

_____

_____

_____

We understand that **Giving Back** is an attribute and quality of God, exemplified by Him, giving His only begotten Son, according to **John 3:16.** "For God so loved the world that he gave his only begotten Son, that whosoever believeth in Him should not perish, but have everlasting life."

There are several keywords in this scripture (John 3:16) that should resonate with us as believers.

Scramble:

1. _ o_ _ o   3. _ orl_   5. _ n_ _
2. _ o_ _d   4. _av_   6. _ _n

"Giving Back" does come naturally to some as it should and is a part of living CHRIST-like, freely giving to others, especially those in need. "Giving Back" sometimes requires sharing meals, providing a bed/shelter, time, effort, energy, and money. To add, a listening ear, prayer, fasting, words of encouragement, showing of support, acknowledgment, and concern for others. The word hospitable comes to mind. Hospitality is a characteristic of God and has a varied association of costs. Sometimes you lose, but "Winning!"

Synonyms of hospitality include accommodation, cheer, companionship, comradeship, consideration, cordiality, friendliness, generosity, good cheer, heartiness, and hospitableness.

Compare these synonyms to the Fruits of the Spirit according to **Galatians 5:22-23.**

Fill in the Blanks:

22 But the fruit of the Spirit is lo_ _, jo_, pe_ _ _, long_ _fferings, gen_ _ _ness, _ _ _dness, f_ _ _ _,
23 Mee_ness, tempe_ _ nance: against such there is no law.

In 3 John (personal note to Gaius), we find that John, the writer, took a liking to Gaius and his habitual habits of showing great hospitality, showing Himself friendly and generous to which his reputation precedes Him. Gaius repetitively showed hospitality to traveling missionaries and teachers of the Gospel of Jesus Christ. Out of this letter was coined the scripture 3 John 1:2, "Beloved, I wish above all things that thou mayest prosper and be in health, even as thy soul prospereth." We often have heard and used it, applying it to ourselves and/or others. Still, truthfully, this is a scripture written to a certain individual by way of a letter to encourage (Gaius) in the faith and in his health. Gaius had shown himself to be hospitable and generously **"Giving Back"** to others noted by John.

In which ways do you fit into this passage?

1. **Gaius - 3 John 1:8 a Fellow-helper of the Truth**
2. **Diotrephes - 3 John 1:9-11 a self-proclaimed church leader that fails to listen to God's word or reflect "Gods values," only looking out for Himself or**
3. **Demetrius - 3 John 1:12 a man of good report that followed the "Truth" in itself!**

As John encouraged Gaius, we should all adopt and abide to practice hospitality, cling to the truth, and do what's right! Show the Love of God for all and be a reflection of Christ **"Giving Back!"**

30

WHAT CAUSES DISCOURAGEMENT

Discouragement - a noun defined as a loss of confidence or enthusiasm; dispiritedness or an attempt to prevent something by showing disapproval or creating difficulties; deterrent.

---

iscouragement - a noun defined as a loss of confidence or enthusiasm; dispiritedness or an attempt to prevent something by showing disapproval or creating difficulties; deterrent.

(4) Cases of Discouragement:

What Causes Discouragement in your life?

1. _____

2. _____

3. _____

4. _____

Scripture Text: Nehemiah 4
Spiritual Integrity
Ephesians 6:10-20

Integrity is defined as having integrity. It means reliably doing the right thing. It's a personality trait we admire since it means a person has a moral compass that doesn't waver. It literally means having "wholeness" of character, just as an integer is a "whole number" with no fractions.

Spiritual is defined as of, relating to, or affecting the human spirit or soul as opposed to material or physical things; of or relating to religion or religious belief.

The opposite of integrity is compartmentalizing your life. The word "integrity" comes from the word "integer," which means a unit of one. It means you don't slice and dice your life like pieces of a pie. Integrity means all parts of your life are integrated together. You act the same no matter where you go. You don't act one way at work, another way at church, and another way with your friends. Integrity is being truthful in every area of your life.

Have you compartmentalized your life? Are there some areas where you lack integrity? God wants you wrapped in the truth. So confess your sins to Him and ask Him to strengthen your ability to live transparently before others.

Hypocrite: Acting a part in a play; pretense of piety; pretender; false or goddess; feigning to be what one is not. John 8:13, Hypocrites; hope; perish. Isaiah 9:17, Hypocrite; evildoer.

What does Spiritual Integrity Mean to you?

_____

_____

_____

_____

_____

What does Spiritual mean by definition:

_____

_____

_____

_____

_____

What does Integrity mean by definition:

_____

_____

_____

_____

_____

Are there some areas where you lack integrity:

_____

_____

_____

_____

_____

31

LETTING GO OF MISERY

(ECCL. 8:6, ECCL. 1-10, JOB 16:2, 11:16)

The Cliché that "Misery Loves Company" is a testament to many; the meaning that people who are unhappy may get some consolation from knowing that others are unhappy too.

---

*S*omething to remember is that Satan is miserable and walks to and forth seeking to ensure that **YOU** are miserable, too.

Understanding that misery, this form of bondage (mental state of slavery), is a "state of mind" fueled by one's inner thoughts, process, or way of thinking.

Precipitated, sometimes by acts that one has experienced in this walk of life, mental status of unhealthy thoughts and negative emotions, sometimes even by genetics or familial genealogy.

By definition, Misery is a state or feeling of great distress or discomfort of mind or body; wretchedness of condition or circumstances; distress or suffering caused by need, privation, or poverty; great mental or emotional distress; extreme unhappiness; a cause or source of distress.

Have we ever looked at the cliché and thought that sometimes individuals do not necessarily want to let go of misery? Sometimes misery is not truly attempting to hold YOU captive as company, but that YOU love to remain in it/or have its company? These questions give the mind the understanding that, in most cases, being miserable is optional. It is a choice! For some, misery can be a way of life and a reflection of individual personalities, characteristics, and/or behaviors.

Can we all agree that everyone goes through something, pitfalls, whether good, bad, indifferent, hurtful, et cetera, in this life? However, we all have choices about how we deal with what we have gone or will go through. The separation between God and Man left space for what we know as sin. But, God by way of Jesus, who gave Himself as a ransom, *1st Timothy 2:6,* came that we might experience liberty, freedom, encouraging us to stand fast, therefore, in the liberty wherewith Christ hath made us free, and be not entangled **again** with the yoke of bondage. *Galatians 5:1.*

The statement that "Life is too important and meaningful to be measured and controlled by the pithy(forceful/brief) clichés" rings out with clarity that by choice through Christ, we can get past things that we thought we would never get over, the state of "letting it go," not to mention we can get past things that we may have to continue to live with. Is it not Paul who was told that God's Grace was sufficient, 1st Corinthians 12:7-10, understanding that removal of the thorn in his flesh was Paul's initial resolution to what he identified as a problem? However, God's refusal to remove Paul's thorn led to continued effectiveness from Paul in ministry; he yet took pleasure in glorifying God. The title of the song it is "Time to Let It Go," shouts volumes. Let's let go of misery and shun its crafty and cunning ways of requesting company!

Replace misery with the fruits of the spirit, Galatians 5:22-23.

Love - 1st Peter 4:8, "And above all things have fervent charity among yourselves: for charity shall cover the multitude of sins."
Joy - Nehemiah 8:10, "For the Joy of the Lord is My Strength."
Peace - Philippians 4:7, And the peace of God "surpasses all understanding," shall keep your hearts and minds through Christ Jesus.
Long-suffering - having or showing patience despite troubles, especially those caused by others.
Gentleness - Psalm 18:35, "Thou hast also given me the shield of thy salvation: and thy right hand hath held me up, and thy gentleness hath made me great."
Goodness - Romans 12:9, "[Let] love be without dissimulation. Abhor that which is evil; cleave to that which is good."
Faith - Hebrew 11:1-2, "Faith shows the reality of what we hope for; it is the evidence of things we cannot see." 2, "Through their faith, the people in days of old earned a good reputation."
Meekness - Matthew 11:29, "Take my yoke upon you, and learn of me; for I am meek and lowly in heart: and ye shall find rest unto your souls."
Temperance - (self-control), 2 Peter 1:6, "And to knowledge, temperance; and to temperance, patience; and to patience, godliness.

Help. Psalm 46:1, God is our refuge and strength, a very present help in the time of trouble.

_____

_____

_____

_____

_____

32

WHEN TO ASK FOR HELP

The word **HELP,** *according to Dictionary.com, is defined as to give or provide what is necessary: to accomplish a task or satisfy a need; contribute strength or means to; render assistance to; cooperate effectively with; aid; assist; to save; rescue; succor: to make easier or less difficult; contribute to; facilitate.*

---

he Bible defines the word Help as follows, to come to one's aid; those who give aid (coworker's) helpful deeds.

Do you find asking for Help to be a struggle? If so, explain briefly why.

Some thoughts or ways of thinking, patterns of thought that impede asking for help: You may feel that you don't need help or that any person offering help is threatening your independence. For example, maybe you have had to look out for yourself from an early age due to neglectful parents. Now you believe suddenly accepting help from others makes you weak.

Perhaps it was instilled in you that an adult or someone your age must take responsibility for Himself. As a result, you believe it is socially wrong to ask (or to be a burden to) friends and family for assistance.

You may battle with fears of rejection or have a tendency towards perfectionism. Both motivations can cause you to avoid accepting help for fear of failing or being seen as a failure.

If you're a business owner or professional, you may be worried that needing help can demonstrate a lack of professionalism.

Consequently, you might feel that someone not handling his own affairs is inferior or incompetent.

WE UNDERSTAND THAT BEING PRIDEFUL IS A SIN, AND BELIEVING WE CAN DO EVERYTHING LEADS TO FAILURE.

Even in the beginning, God saw that Adam needed some help. So he created a helper that was suitable for Adam, **Genesis 2:18.**

When you think beyond the surface of the simple word or topic concerning the word HELP, you may begin accepting that the term Help is extremely challenging for all of us at one time or another. It can be especially hard for those of us who believe that seeking help undermines our independence and ability to cope. "EXPOSURE OF ONE'S OWN INSECURITIES," "STRUGGLES OF INADEQUACY," places us on paths of detriment to ourselves and others. Many times, making yourself aloof (not friendly or forthcoming; cool and distant) from other human beings, you are building an invisible barrier around yourself that wards off the potential for new relationships and friendships.

Moreover, by refusing to accept help, we disregard the fact that we are social beings who need to cooperate with one another to thrive. Hence, we all need a little **HELP** sometimes! Ephesians 4:32, *"And be ye kind one to another, tenderhearted, forgiving one another, even as God for Christ's sake hath forgiven you."* The question is will you allow God to ____ ____ ____ ____ you?

In Exodus 4:1, we see that Moses struggled with his insecurities/inadequacies. Let's look at some. (4:1) They will not believe me. What others think of us often discourages our asking for HELP. Many people do not move forward in God because they feel they will not be received by people. (4:1), "For they will say the Lord hath not appeared unto thee." Often, the criticism of our own (prideful thoughts/bad/ flawed thinking) will push us into an abortion of God's said/instructed mission. (4:10), "I am not eloquent, neither heretofore, nor since thou hast spoken unto they servant: but I am slow of speech, and of a slow tongue." Moses refused the help that God was providing even after several examples given by God. Moses' fears of being inadequate superseded the power God had displayed to Him, thus, leading to God's anger being kindled towards Him. (4:14), "And the anger of the Lord was kindled against Moses, and he said, Is not Aaron, the Levite, thy brother? I know that he can speak well. And, behold, he cometh forth to meet thee; and when he seeth thee, he will be glad in his heart."

While there is nothing impossible through God, we see that Moses struggled to buy into that, and he asked God for HELP.

It is possible to change your thinking and become more receptive to help in the future with the understanding that God sends help in all different ways: Yourself, Himself, situations, occurrences, people, places, and things when you help others.

Allow the relationship of reciprocation to abide, meaning if you help others, then allow for others to help YOU!

Remember that sometimes help does not come in the form you want, but **HELP** comes. Sometimes HELP does not come when you want it, but HELP comes. Know who task for HELP. Beware of your individual areas of expertise!

Learn to trust others. Modify your expectations. Remember that people are only human and have both good and bad traits.

Recognize that disappointment, fear, abandonment, and rejection are possible in all human relationships.

Find yourself worthy and capable of making wise decisions and being around decent people; in this case, people of God, and when in need, ask for **H E L P!** Be open and ready. Avoid second guessing if you should take the HELP sent by GOD! **"BE STRONG ENOUGH TO STAND ALONE, SMART ENOUGH TO KNOW WHEN YOU NEED HELP, AND BRAVE ENOUGH TO ASK FOR IT!"**

"Now unto Him that is able to do exceedingly and abundantly above all that we could ask or think, according to his Power that worketh in us," Ephesians 3:20.

_____
_____
_____
_____
_____
_____
_____
_____
_____
_____
_____
_____
_____

33

LEARN TO ENCOURAGE YOURSELF

Some days of feeling down, dis-encouraged, depressed, tired, confused, the list can go on and on: "I'm just feeling some type of way."

---

or these are natural attributes of thoughts and emotions. God forbid that we dwell there. Not being alone, I'm sure we have all been there at one point or another. As the cliché goes, "Just keep on living." If you have not experienced these thoughts, feelings, or emotions just yet, you will! "For all scripture is given by the inspiration of God, and is profitable for doctrine, for reproof, for correction, for instruction in righteousness. That the man of God may be perfect, thoroughly furnished unto all good works." (2nd Timothy 3:16-17).

God encouraged me to find myself in these thoughts and emotions today through seeking Him and prayer. Self-Encouragement! A vital tool that comes from within. What we all need in this race, this war of spiritual battle!

- Encourage- give support, confidence, or hope.
- Learn to talk to yourself the right way.
- Learn how to quote God's promises. We must study the word of God to know His promises. Study to show thyself approved unto God, a workman that needeth not to be ashamed, rightly dividing the word of truth (2nd Timothy 2:15).
- Learn how to pray for yourself - Love Yourself. Love this Great Commandment, "And thou shalt love the Lord thy God with all thy heart, and with all thy soul, and with all thy mind, and with all thy strength: this is the first commandment." And the second is, like, namely this, "Thou shalt love thy neighbour as thyself. There is none other commandment greater than these." (Mark 12:30-31)
- Psalm 30:5 - For his anger endureth but a moment. In his favor is life. Weeping may endure for a night but joy cometh in the morning.
- Your Joy will return! God promised it! A promise of God, "The world didn't give it, so the world cannot take my Joy away!"

What did not destroy me will only make me STRONGER! After evil by his brothers, the accusation of Potiphar's wife, the butler's neglect, and seven years of famine, Joseph encouraged Himself with trust in God, knowing that what was meant for evil, God transformed it into Good! Genesis 50:20, "But as for you, ye thought evil against me; but God meant it unto good, to bring to pass, as it is this day, to save much people alive."

Speak life to your dead situations.

Learn to encourage yourself in the Lord!

34

DO NOT BE DEFEATED BY THE ADVERSITIES OF THIS LIFE

During times of the pitfalls of life, one can become overwhelmed, subdued by the barriers of some sort that present themselves, and often stop progression or you from "MOVING FORWARD."

Have you ever been there? Care to share?

_____

_____

_____

Because greater is he that is within you than he
that is in the world.

— *1 JOHN 4:4*

Often these "Pitfalls" or "Valley of Lows" leave many dejected in a whirlwind of the snowball effect, often given into uttering the phrase "one thing after another." I might add to that the statement the infamous "If it ain't one thing, then it's another." Do those sound familiar? Please remember, **"The power of death and life lies in the power of your tongue,"** **Proverbs 18:21.**

These statements represent an attitude, a pattern of such a way of thinking, and patterns of thoughts that are negative and often linked to pessimism. These thoughts cloud the eyes of your future and are clear thoughts of evil and untruths. So let's define the word **Pessimism.**

1. The tendency to see, anticipate or emphasize only bad or undesirable outcomes, results, conditions, problems, et cetera.
2. The doctrine that the existing world is the worst of all possible worlds or that all things naturally tend to be evil.
3. The belief that the evil and pain in the world are not compensated for by goodness and happiness.

When looking at that definition, we can identify with the thoughts of pessimism and understand how an individual engages in pessimistic behaviors or patterns of thoughts.

For example, one who expresses hopelessness denounces their own capabilities, are reluctant to take the risk, refuse to take steps toward personal development or growth, and utters nothing you do will make a difference in particular circumstances. Does any of these pertain to you?

_____

_____

_____

_____

_____

It's Great, to be HONEST! It's the BEST RESOLVE to getting HELP!

According to Dr. Paul Meier, a Christian psychiatrist, "Attitudes are nothing more than habits of thought, and habits can be acquired," meaning it is not "just the way you are." "An act repeated becomes an attitude realized." So, this means you can change your way of thinking and adjust your attitude, which will be reflected in your behavioral outcomes.

John wrote with the certainty and understanding that this will be a dilemma for many, **"Ye are of God, little children, and have overcome them: because greater is he that is within you, than he that is in the world." (1 John 4:4).**

Observation and interpretation allow us to identify with the ability to overcome in this scripture along with application in the scripture, concluding that this is done by the power of God that lies inside you. In other words, apply the Power of Overcoming. Let's self-check this.

1. Be honest with your steps to conquering pessimism. Try allowing selected individuals in your circle of life to point out the onslaught of those behaviors of negativity, i.e., that trait of complaining.
2. Avoid the company of negativity at all costs. Your input in negativity should be "NAY." The Bible **says to shun(abstain) from the very appearance of evil, 1ˢᵗ (Thessalonians 5:22).** Be wise in the selection of your immediate circle, seek after those that are positive, show love, and exhibit wisdom. Solomon writes in *Psalm 13:20, "He that walketh with wise men shall be wise: but a companion of fools shall be destroyed."*
3. Be a servant, especially to those of less fortune. The ability to serve others allows for the acts of humility to be a driven mode or motive of operation, thus

creating positive feelings, enacting your sense of
value, and increasing self-worth.

4. Seek after the good in every circumstance presented
   to you. This is a true enactment of *Romans 8:28 in
   action, "And we know that all things work together for
   good to them that love God, to them who are the called
   according to his purpose."*

Joseph came to this revelation in Genesis 50:20, "What the
devil meant for evil against me, God meant it for my good."

Job had a plethora of evil against Him, but thoughts of
pessimism were not the resolution. Although clearly, I'm sure
the spirit showed itself. Still, optimistically Job said, "Naked
came I out of my mother's womb, and naked shall I return
thither: The Lord gave, and the Lord hath taken away; blessed
be the name of the Lord," Job 1:21.

Job 14:14, "If a man die, shall he live again? All the days of
my appointed time will I wait, till my change come."

President Harry S. Truman stated, "A pessimist is one who
makes difficulties of his opportunities and an optimist is one
who makes opportunities of his difficulties."

Face to Face, Toe to Toe with difficulty or adversities, see the
playground for what it is: engaging in the rules of optimistic
opportunities. Stand in the midst of it all with a clear
understanding of who holds your future. Be not dismayed nor
Perplexed. "Do Not Be Defeated; But Overcome and Conquer
because greater is he that is within you, than he that is in the
world." (1 John 4:4).

Keep the "Eye of the Tiger." **Find God in EVERYTHING.**

Eye of the Tiger by Survivor

Rising up, back on the street
Did my time, took my chances
Went the distance, now I'm back on my feet
Just a man and his will to survive

So many times it happens too fast
You change your passion for glory
Don't lose your grip on the dreams of the past
You must fight just to keep them alive

It's the eye of the tiger
It's the thrill of the fight
Rising up to the challenge of our rival
And the last known survivor
Stalks his prey in the night
And he's watching us all with the eye of the tiger

Face to face, out in the heat
Hanging tough, staying hungry
They stack the odds 'til we take to the street
For the kill with the skill to survive

It's the eye of the tiger

1st Kings 2:1-12
2nd Timothy 3:16,17

_____
_____
_____
_____
_____

ABOUT THE AUTHOR

Pastor Tekisha D. Wimbush is a Native of Cleveland, Ohio. She is a minister of the Gospel of Jesus Christ and the wife of Bishop Willie J. Wimbush Jr., Church of the Reform Church of Love in Cleveland, Ohio.

Lady Wimbush's commitment to serving and helping others is evident through her lifestyle of service and dedication to the families and communities she serves. She diligently works with the Women's Ministry at Church of the Reform Church of Love to promote unity and sisterhood. She frequently hosts prayer and Women's Forum meetings, retreats, workshops, and other events to empower women to develop and grow in the love of God. In addition, Lady Wimbush serves in various ministries within The Church of the Reform, including Adult Sunday School Teacher, Church Finance/Administration Committee, Praise Team, Engagement / Program Coordinator, Youth Ministry, and Outreach.

Lady Wimbush has a 15-year history of employment with a Social Service agency in Cleveland, Ohio, where she supervised for over seven years. Lady Wimbush currently serves as a Licensed Social Worker for a Cleveland Hospice Agency, providing supportive comfort care. She also provides Clinical Counseling at a Cleveland Counseling Agency.

She holds multiple Master's Degrees in Social Work and Early Childhood Education and a Bachelor's Degree in Business Administration and Social Science. Lady Wimbush has a heart that resonates with restoring family relationships in a holistic modality. Lady Wimbush engages with both Macro and Micro community outreach to coordinate services to support those in need.

With all her accomplishments, she still considers supporting her husband in ministry and raising God-fearing children her primary purpose. As a mother of three, now adult, children, she firmly affirms that the best way to raise successful children is to be an active role model in demonstrating the love and fear of the Lord, which is the beginning of Wisdom.

TekishaDWimbush.com

 facebook.com/TekishaDWimbush
 instagram.com/tekishadwimbush